D1396481

HIGH FINANCE ON A LOW BUDGET

by Mark Skousen

Since no two people are alike, the advice contained in this guidebook may not be suitable for all investors. You should send for, and carefully read, any prospectuses or other information before committing funds to any investment vehicle. The information herein has been carefully compiled from sources believed to be reliable, but because of changing laws and events, the author cannot guarantee its accuracy. Nor can the author guarantee the performance of such investments. He believes that his investment approach is sound, but cannot be held responsible for actions taken by purchasers of this book. The first rule of investing is, "*caveat emptor* — let the buyer beware!*"

Mark Skousen
P. O. Box 611
Merrifield, VA 22116

TO OUR CHILDREN

Valerie, Timothy, and Leslie Ann

ACKNOWLEDGEMENTS

Finding ways for the small investor to participate in the world of high finance has been a fruitful and rewarding effort. It would not have been possible without the help of dozens of financial counselors, brokers, and investors. Over the past years, as an investment counselor myself, I've learned a great deal about the needs of the small investor who fights daily against the ravages of taxes and inflation.

First and foremost, I would like to pay tribute to my wife, Jo Ann, for her painstaking efforts to edit and rewrite portions of the manuscript that may not have seemed clear the first time around. When the work was finally complete, she showed me how little original material was mine and jokingly suggested that she be the sole author! But I was able to bribe her with the promise that if *I* could remain the author, she could get all the royalties. . . . I may have second thoughts next year!

Thanks also to Howard Ruff for writing the introduction, and for showing a keen interest in the plight of the small investor; to Adrian Day, managing editor of *Personal Finance*, for providing much-needed leads and information; to Kathe Green for verifying the addresses and telephone numbers of the firms mentioned in the book; and to Benjamin Franklin, fondly known as "Poor Richard," for providing some illustrious quotations at the beginning of each chapter.

MARK SKOUSEN

TABLE OF CONTENTS

INTRODUCTION:
ONLY FOR THE RICH?
By Howard J. Ruff

Recently I was interviewed on a radio station in Chicago with an audience of mostly poor people. The thrust of the host's questions implied that I was a bad guy because I didn't have any good suggestions to help the poor beat inflation. That is sort of like killing the messenger who brings the bad news that the cards are marked, the dice are loaded and the odds are rigged, and the house wins most of the time. Why blame me because I can't answer a question which has no answer?

If I write about apartment buildings or diamonds, and you don't have enough money to buy one, you could understandably react by feeling frustrated and mad, and I'm a convenient target for your rage. I understand that, but it really isn't quite rational.

The mythical "average" investor may be in his late 40s, has two to three years of a college education, and makes around $35,000 a year. He has between $10,000 and $50,000 in savings and investments, and an inflated equity in his home. It wasn't many years ago that he would have been considered one of the more affluent members of society. Now he is almost lower-middle class, and government is taking a larger and larger portion of his income as he gets ratcheted into higher tax brackets and inflation is devastating the traditional investments that he is making (i.e., blue chip stocks, bonds, CDs, cash value insurance, etc.). He has this hard, cold knot of fear in his stomach warning him that the affluence he pursued and thought he had found, is turning to ashes in his hands, and his retirement will be nothing better than genteel poverty.

I try to serve a broad spectrum of investors. There are thousands of you whose assets and income fall well below the mythical "average" investor. There are also people who have assets in the millions of dollars. By the same token, there are a lot of little old ladies on social security who are also asking me for help.

Actually, the less you have, the more important financial advice is to you. The rich can better afford to make expensive mistakes and recover from them. Most people would be just as happy on $5 millon as on $10 million if they lost half of it. But if they only had $5,000 and lost half, they would be devastated.

My most important objective is the preservation of whatever you have, as opposed to the aggressive accumulation of wealth. The insidious nature of inflation is that you lose purchasing power while numbers appear to be growing. You can get raises and capital gains that, after taxes and inflation, actually result in large losses of purchasing power, while generating phony taxable "profits."

I have awakened a lot of people in this country to this sick situation. The rich can afford the expensive attorneys and estate planners. The middle and lower-middle class can't afford that kind of advice. I believe that we have helped those people to have insights into their planning which can help them avoid these costly hidden mistakes.

Let's look at another typical misconception—that the advice to buy gold and silver can only be followed by wealthy people.

You can buy one Krugerrand for a little over $700. You can buy a $\frac{1}{10}$ Krugerrand for about $80. You can buy a roll of American silver dimes for around $70. You can buy food storage, one bucket of wheat at a time, for approximately $18 a bucket (45 lbs).

Just because you can't do everything, or do it all at once, is no excuse for doing nothing or being angry.

Let's list all the things that you could do if you had $5,000.

1. You could start accumulating some food storage.

2. You could buy silver coins—a roll, or a partial bag.

3. You could buy some bullion-type gold coins ($80 to $700 each).

4. You could become a collector of inexpensive semiprecious stones, baseball cards, comic books, or numismatic coins.

5. You could grow a garden and become self-sufficient and independent, drying your produce in your oven or in the sun. There are books which show you exactly how to do it.

6. You could become politically involved and try to bring about change. You can ring doorbells or stuff envelopes for the campaign of some free-market, honest-money oriented candidate who might help to bring about some change. Ultimately that might do you more good than having all the gold and silver in the world.

7. If you have an unutilized inflated equity in a home, you can borrow against it and put it to work with a beat-inflation program.

8. You could have bought a few government bonds recently when they were cheap—enjoying a 12 percent interest plus the chance for capital gains.

What couldn't you do if you had only $5,000? You couldn't buy a good one-carat diamond, and you probably would find it difficult to buy a big apartment house. But using Al Lowry's creative finance ideas as described in his book and mine, you can go out with only a few thousand dollars and make a downpayment on a small house or duplex, fix it up, raise the rent and the market value, and trade for a bigger property. Great real estate pyramids have been built on less than $5,000. We have a marvelous opportunity for creative financing in this disrupted marketplace that is now a buyer's paradise.

If you think you have limitations and can't take good advice, the wild dogs of inflation and economic disruption may bite you, and you may die financially. If I do nothing more than persuade you that you can spread your wings, you just might save your financial life.

I salute my friend Mark Skousen for expanding on this important theme in his new book, *HIGH FINANCE ON A LOW BUDGET*. His unique "$100 investment portfolio" proves that anyone, no matter how small his savings, can protect himself from the ravages of inflation and taxes. Mark has a great gift for clear and honest prose, a rare gift. I strongly urge you to read this book, and profit from Mark's sound advice.

HOWARD J. RUFF

CHAPTER 1

WELCOME TO THE WORLD OF HIGH FINANCE

"He that would catch fish, must venture his bait."

As a financial writer and consultant, I receive hundreds of letters each year from concerned investors. One of the most frequent letters I receive goes something like this:

> "Your advice is fine for the wealthy.' But what about those of us living on a *limited* budget—the wage-earners, retirees, housewives, students, and widows who have only a few thousand dollars, or less, to invest? How can we beat inflation and taxes like the rich do?"

In these troubled times of raging inflation, rising taxes and economic crises, millions of investors are coming to the painful conclusion that "it takes money to make money." The rags-to-riches story of Horatio Alger has only a million-to-one chance of recurring in today's harsh world. The small saver seems destined to a low-yielding savings account that is rapidly being devoured by taxes and inflation.

In the past, the world of high finance has been virtually closed to the small investor, who doesn't have thousands of dollars with which to meet minimum investment requirements. The wealthy can take advantage of highly leveraged tax shelters to avoid paying Uncle Sam. They can afford sophisticated money managers who profit from "inside" information on gold, silver, and commodities. They participate in exotic foreign investments, overseas banking, and money havens.

In the end, while the rich get richer, the poor get poorer. The true victims of this rich man's game have been the millions of average, middle-class citizens who bear the brunt of costly living and inequitable taxation.

Small Investors Can Escape

In response to the small investor's plight, I began to research *low-cost* ways for the novice investor to preserve and increase his capital. In preparing this material, I searched for inflation hedges and tax shelters that would accept small investments of as little as $100—and sometimes even less. I have discovered ways that *anyone* with a little money, a little knowledge, and a little courage can start down the road to high finance. I can't promise instant fortunes, but I can foresee a comfortable nest egg in just a couple of years. You can invest just like a millionaire even if you have less than $1,000, and I'll show you exactly how to do it in this book. Little known, but effective, tools *are* finally available to the "penny capitalist" in the lucrative fields of hard money, real estate, commodities, the stock market, and foreign investments.

This book offers specific how-to information for the small investor, including names, addresses, and minimum requirements of reputable companies. In addition, it explains how individual investment markets work, when to get out of one investment and into another, and how to minimize your tax liability on your newly-found wealth. Soon you will have the confidence to be your own investment advisor, and to help you get started, I have included specific portfolio recommendations in a later chapter. These diversified portfolios will help you get started and will assure that you have a good balance. There is even a $100 portfolio, for those who are really on a low budget!

How to Get Started

Of course, you may be among the thousands or even millions of Americans who have trouble saving $5, let alone $500. You may be reading this book not just for the "high finance" but for the "low budget" as well. If so, the next chapter is a must for you. It will show you some simple but powerful techniques for lowering your *cost* of living without lowering your *standard* of living, and thereby show you how to create some start-up investment capital immediately.

When dealing in small amounts, commissions and fees become critical. The well-to-do investor can afford to pay substantial fees, but the small investor cannot. Therefore, in my research for this book, I have tried to emphasize low commissions and fees as an essential ingredient. For example, there are reputable coin dealers who buy and sell gold and silver at the lowest possible premiums. Incorporating can be done for $100. Tax-free municipal bonds can be purchased without paying a commission. And common stocks and high-grade corporate bonds can be obtained *without* a broker and *without* paying commissions! This book is full of similar examples.

Two Roads to Financial Independence

In a famous poem, Robert Frost speaks of "two roads," one well traveled, the other less traveled. The same is true in the financial world. Traditionally there are two approaches to increasing one's wealth. The first approach relies on expanding one's *income level.* Many distinguished books have been written that tell you how to ask for a raise, how to land a higher-paying job, or how to make a killing in real estate, mail order, or some other sideline business. Unfortunately, this method simply doesn't work for many people, especially during a recessionary climate.

The second approach is not so common, but in my opinion, it is just as effective. Rather than having to earn more, this approach simply requires you to spend less! It involves systematically cutting one's spending and thereby increasing one's *savings*. Save more, and invest it wisely. This approach may seem more difficult because it hinges upon your self-control. Your success depends entirely upon your own actions, and not upon the actions of others who must give you a raise, a new job, a contract on a house, or an inheritance. Just as staying on a diet requires willpower and determination, so does sticking within a budget require those same traits.

Successful investing and financial freedom involve two steps, *know-how* and a *willingness to save*. It is impossible to make wealth *and keep it* without these two qualities. The wise investor, no matter what his level of income, will save as much as possible. While wealthy individuals do spend lots of money, they save even more. If they didn't, they would soon lose their millions. Millionaires do go bankrupt if they fall into bad spending habits, and never learn to control their spending until it's too late. This is especially true when they've come into their wealth suddenly! That's why the next chapter, on budgeting, is essential to beating inflation. No matter how much you make, if you fail to save and to budget your income, you won't break away from the crowd.

It Can Be Done

Every year thousands of savvy novice investors do break away from the pack and turn a meager income into a small fortune. Every one of these success stories has one thing in common: *each had access to the formula used by the wealthy to make spectacular profits.*

Recently I saw an article in a newspaper that read: "Two Akron charities will each receive half of a $1 million estate from a retired General Tire Co. worker who never made more than $15,000 annually."

If this man could do it, you can, too!

A young friend of mine also knows the formula for high finance on a low budget. He has always been a careful investor. He has never made much money on his salary, nor has he inherited any money from relatives. Yet he has over $25,000 of investment funds, accrued gradually over the years through a variety of investments in stocks, bonds, and gold and silver coins.

Thousands of similar cases occur every year, and not just by chance. High finance is possible and predictable even for the small investor making less than $10,000 a year. The steps outlined in the next few chapters will show you the way.

CHAPTER 2

HOW TO GET STARTED
—THE EASY WAY
TO BUDGET

*"Women & wine, game & deceit, make the
wealth small and the wants great."*

The problem with most household budgets is that they are
usually planned backwards. Most people figure up how much
they need to spend, for such necessities as rent, food, clothing,
insurance, credit cards, and medical bills, and then plan to save
whatever is left over. The trouble with this plan is that in today's
inflated economy, nothing is ever left over, except maybe last
night's vegetables. In reality this is no budget at all! No matter
how much you think you are cutting down, something will
always come up toward the end of the month. And if you
have that money in your checking account, you'll probably
spend it. If you don't plan ahead to put aside a *specific amount*
of money for savings each month, nothing will ever be put
aside.

Why Savings Is the Key

Studies have demonstrated that at every income level, a certain
number of individuals are able to maintain a savings program.
Conversely, a certain number of individuals in every group are

constantly deep in debt. It doesn't matter whether you choose a group of millionaires, average wage-earners, or low-income families; in every group, you'll find a great disparity of spending and savings habits. To be sure, the savers are far outnumbered by the borrowers. But while the vast majority stay deeply in debt and can hardly make ends meets, there is always that small minority who consistently succeed in building a workable investment program.

The disparity becomes even more evident when viewed on a world level. Most foreigners are far more conscious of saving money than are Americans. They save incredible amounts of money on *less* income than even the lowest-paid American. I observed this phenomenon many times while living in Latin America—the Latins would cut spending to the bone in order to save money for an automobile or appliance costing *three times* what we would typically pay—and they didn't use credit.

On the other side of the world, the Japanese have an average income level about equal to that in the U. S., although the cost of living is generally higher in Japan. Yet the average savings rate is 30 percent in Japan! Compare this to the U. S., where the rate has fallen to a miserable 6 percent. How is it possible for one group of people to earn the same amount of money as another, yet save remarkably more money? The answer is obvious, yet bears repeating: they spend less.

Thus, we see that the amount of money you save can be completely unrelated to your income. It isn't so much the amount you make that counts, but how you choose to spend it. Most Americans are extravagant by the world's standards. Once you recognize this fact—that you are *wasting* money every day of the year—you'll quickly discover how relatively painless it is to begin a savings program.

Eliminating waste and increasing savings is the only sound road to financial independence. Merely increasing your take-home pay won't guarantee the end of your money problems, as evidenced by the number of high-income families that are just barely getting by. You probably know yourself how quickly a raise is assimilated into your day-to-day spending patterns. A recent magazine article showed how a family with an income of $38,000 a year was "struggling" to make ends meet. Living in Washington, D. C., we've met numerous Congressmen who complain how meager their $65,000 salary is. Needless to say, these high-income people don't know the right way to budget.

The Right Way to Budget

Step #1: Put Savings First. I have found that there are four simple steps to a sound budget program. To me, the cardinal principle, and the rule that must be immutable in your life, is this: *savings come first.* Before the rent, before taxes, even before food for your children, savings have to be first and foremost on your list of priorities. As harsh as this counsel may seem, I guarantee it works!

How much should you save? I have found that the optimum amount to begin saving is 10 percent of your income. Eventually you will be able to save more, but 10 percent is simple to compute, it's regular, and it automatically adjusts for changes in your income. It is particularly useful for salesmen, consultants, and others whose paychecks vary widely from month to month. This "tithing" principle can work for anyone. Even if you're a student with a $35 allowance, you can manage to set aside $3.50 for long-term savings.

A word of caution is in order however. As you watch your savings grow, perhaps for the first time in your life, you may feel tempted to spend it. Perhaps the car breaks down, or you want a vacation, or you should pay off some installment loans. After all, it's your money! But you must not yield to these temptations. Of course, you should have an area in your budget for short-term savings which will be available for emergencies and household extras. But your investment portfolio is a *long-term* savings plan, and none of it should be touched until it has been socked away, earning you a high rate of return, for several years.

The Virtues and Vice of Automatic Withholding

The savings-first method is not new, of course. Many small investors have eliminated the temptation of spending their savings by never seeing it in the first place. They arrange to have their savings taken out of their paychecks, before they ever see the money. Plans include corporate matching-share plans, automatic purchase of government savings bonds, and over-withholding of federal and state income taxes. The concept of automatic withholding is absolutely sound. Unfortunately, however, most of the vehicles available to the salary-earner are poor inflation hedges. Blue chip stocks have suffered and declined in value in real and nominal terms over the past decade or more. Government savings bonds offer a return that is lower than the current rate of inflation. And in the case of over-withholding of taxes, you're lending your savings to the government interest-free! In forthcoming chapters, I will show you some far better ways to invest your savings.

Putting savings first will undoubtedly put pressure on your spending habits. This is exactly what it is meant to do—to force you to budget. You're still presumedly making the same amount of income, so now that you're using more of it to save, you have less to spend. Unless you cut back somewhere, you'll end up further into consumer debt, which is the road to disaster. Budgeting your money is the key to a successful savings plan and financial freedom.

There are almost as many budget theories around as there are diet plans. You may already be utilizing one with some degree of success. Many give the reader specific guidelines, telling you what percentage of your income should be spent for food, housing, car repairs, entertainment, etc. The problem with this approach is that no two people and no two families are alike. You may have a health problem that requires you to spend more than the allotted percentage for medical expenses, while the fact that you garden may greatly reduce the percentage you spend on food. Similarly, if your car breaks down you can't very well wait until it fits into your budget to get it fixed. While it can be very helpful to compare your expenditures with those of an "ideal" budget plan, be careful that you don't end up spending more than you need simply because "the book allows it."

Your Budget Book

Step #2: Write down everything you spend in a budget book. Before you can begin writing up a budget, you must first find out how much you have actually been spending. You will be surprised at how revealing this is. Once you have established your spending pattern, you can tailor a budget to your personal needs. I often recommend the purchase of a simple expense record book to get started. (Hallmark sells an excellent household budget book.) At first, ignore the section that says, "Amount Budgeted," and simply use the section marked "Amount Spent." Then keep a meticulous record of every expenditure you make, every single day. No expenditure is too small to be mentioned, so there's no cheating allowed!

The benefits of such a simple procedure are significant. By making an accurate record of your own personal habits, priorities, and pitfalls, you are able to see exactly what your spending attitudes are, regardless of what some arbitrary budgeter might say they *should* be. Most people tell me they are amazed finally to discover the answer to that age-old question,

"Where did all my money go?"

Now this record can be used to write up your budget allocations for the coming year, making allowances for inflation, another child, and other changing needs. Continue to write down all your expenditures, both to make sure you are sticking to your budget and also to facilitate reassessment of your budget plan as needed.

Step #3: Establish Strict Spending Limitations. Once you have reviewed your spending habits for two or three months, it's time to establish your own, tailor-made budget. List all your expenditures in one of four columns, as follows:

(1) Fixed Expenditures
(2) Necessities
(3) Nice Things to Have
(4) Totally Frivolous Spending

By eliminating all items in the final category, you should be able to find instant money painlessly for your most important "fixed expenditure"—savings. You must decide at the outset that at least 10 percent of your money will go into long-term savings. If emergencies come up, they are paid for by cutting back on any of the other categories, or by dipping into your *short-term* emergency savings account, which is intended for that rainy day that seems to happen every month.

Fixed Expenditures, in addition to your long-term savings program, might include the rent or mortgage payment, car payments, tuition, and other regular monthly payments. You probably should include payment to an emergency fund here, to be used for unexpected repairs, annual vacation, and other expensive but infrequent items.

Necessities might include utilities, food, clothing, gasoline, household needs, medical expenses, and unexpected expenses. Here you must make an important distinction between "needs" and "wants." While these kinds of expenses are absolutely necessary, the amounts you spend on them can vary widely.

You *can* cut back on your driving; you *can* reduce the amount of meat you eat. Much waste can be eliminated without much pain.

Nice Things to Have is just what it sounds like—movies, magazines, extra clothing, eating out, and other items that make life more enjoyable but that you could live without. Look for ways to cut down in these areas, without cutting them out.

Totally Frivolous Spending, as I said, should be eliminated. You should find that the very fact that you are listing every single expenditure will serve to limit your spending. Impulse purchases become less frequent with the knowledge that they will be recorded on the budget and reviewed by members of the household. Those frivolous, unplanned expenditures take an enormous bite out of most disposable incomes, with relatively little satisfaction realized.

Helpful Tips

Reassess your budget from time to time. Perhaps you can find additional ways to cut back and increase your savings beyond the 10 percent level. But don't make the mistake that Congress does when it prepares a national budget. If legislators decide on a new defense or social program, they simply write it into the budget, with little thought as to where the money will come from. It's no wonder that the national debt is $1 trillion, and inflation is soaring. You and I can't print more money when we run out at the end of the month, so we have to take a more prudent approach.

Every column in your budget can be reduced by proper planning. Even the "fixed expenditure" column isn't really fixed in the long run. Perhaps you can lower your rent or mortgage payment by moving, even if only temporarily. A used car can be considerably cheaper than a new car. Life insurance premiums can be cut sharply by shopping for inexpensive term policies while still maintaining needed coverage. You can think of other ways as well. Here are some helpful tips that should be in the small investor's tool kit.

Buy top-quality second-hand items. You can purchase good quality second-hand products at a tremendous discount over retail. Don't hesitate to bargain, especially if a high-ticket item is at stake.

A late-model used car can offer you all the comforts and "newness" of a new car while saving you thousands of dollars. Recently the Hertz Rent-A-Car corporation completed a study on used-car economics. The following chart compares the savings you obtain over a new model, based on the age of the used car. The survey took into account both the price of the car and operating expenses over a three-year period.

Age of Used Car At Purchase	*Percent Savings Over New Car Costs Kept for 3 Years*
1 Year	10%
2 Years	30%
3 Years	48%
4 Years	51%
5 Years	52%
6 Years	53%
7 Years	53%

Based on the Hertz study, clearly the greatest marginal savings is on the 2-to-3-year old used cars. Obviously, the older cars would cost less, but if you want to strike a balance between reducing operating costs and enjoying the luxury of a new car, the best buy is a used car only 2-3 years old. After that, it makes little difference whether you buy a car 4 years old or 7 years old.

The classified section of the newspaper is the best place to shop for a used car, not the local used car dealer. When you purchase a car in the classifieds, you are able to meet the owner, and you can find out a lot about his driving habits and the car's past performance. In most cases, a used car dealer knows little about the previous owners of the cars on his lot. Additionally, the dealer must meet overhead expenses, while the actual owner has only the cost of the ad to cover.

Appliances and other high-ticket items can also be purchased through the classifieds at considerable savings.

Life Insurance

You can also save tremendously on your life insurance premiums by shopping carefully. The low-budget household can seldom afford whole-life or cash-value insurance, but it's surprising how much whole life insurance is sold to the public by high-pressure insurance agents. For the vast majority of investors, *term* insurance is the least expensive and best way to get the life insurance you need to cover your family in case of an untimely death.

But even term insurance rates vary widely from one company to another. I've seen first-year premiums on a $100,000 term policy for a 35-year-old run from $145 to nearly $300! Watch out, too, for insurance policies that charge a very low premium the first year to get you to sign up—and then hit you with much higher premiums afterwards. It's best to use an *independent* insurance agent who can offer you the lowest-priced policy from among numerous insurance companies. The term insurance industry continues to come out with cheaper policies every year, but currently the least expensive rates for 20-year policies are available from Bankers National (for smokers), and Security Mutual (for nonsmokers), according to Joseph Rosenblith & Associates, a company which rates the term policies of the top 220 Best-rated insurance companies.

Impulse Buying

Avoid capricious purchases at garage sales or auctions. It's a great temptation to buy impulsively at a bargain sale. "Bargain" has jokingly been defined as "something you don't need at a price you can't afford to pass up!" Don't become a collector of junk. If you stick to the items you planned on buying *before* you arrived at the garage sale or auction, you will always come out ahead.

The cost of second-hand consumer products is extremely low at garage sales—an average 15 percent of the retail price, even on slightly used items!

Even more valuable than garage sales are the many second-hand stores springing up across the country. They either purchase or take consignments of used goods, reselling them at a modest mark-up. You gain the advantage of a wider selection than can generally be found at garage sales or in the classifieds, and you also have a legitimate, ongoing business to turn to in case something is seriously wrong with your purchase.

Borrow judiciously. It pays to borrow on some high-ticket items, but don't use your credit card for routine purchases. This is another area where you need to examine your shopping habits objectively. Debt can be compared to alcohol in that some people can use it moderately with no ill effects, others avoid it entirely as a matter of principle, and still others become addicted to it until it ruins their lives. Many people prefer using credit cards to carrying large sums of cash. By keeping a running total throughout the month they are able to stay within their budgets, paying the entire bill at the end of the month. But it takes a lot of planning and self control. If you are just getting started on the road to high finance, you should probably put away your plastic money for a while and use your credit only for those items that are rapidly increasing in price, or are high priced such as your home or car.

Incidentally, interest rates on consumer loans vary extensively, so shop around. Check out rates at banks, credit unions, and savings institutions. I once did a survey several years ago on interest rates for cash advances and credit cards—the rates ranged from zero to 24 percent!

High-return Savings

Step #4: Invest your long-term savings in proven inflation hedges.
The fourth step to financial independence is critical. A consistent 10 percent savings layaway plan isn't enough. To build rapidly, you have to depend on investment vehicles that profit from inflation.

Unfortunately, the typical savings account offered by banks, savings and loan associations, credit unions, and major corporations simply can't fulfill this important step.

Investments to Avoid

● *Whole life insurance policies* don't beat inflation. Even the most optimistic surveys show that cash values don't increase more than 6-7 percent a year, far below the inflation rate. Insurance agents may try to get you to pay on a monthly basis, encouraging you to use it as a "forced savings" plan. But the cash values will never build rapidly—and that's what you need. You don't want 6-7 percent a year, you want returns that will double or triple the inflation rate!

● *Bank certificates of deposit* don't keep ahead of inflation, either. Bank CDs do have the virtue of imposing a small penalty for early withdrawal, so you are less likely to dip into your savings, but the return simply isn't high enough. The return is typically linked to U. S. Treasury bill rates, and while T-bills rise and fall with the inflation rate, they seldom exceed it.

● *Government savings bonds* are a poor investment by any

standard. With government waste at an all-time high, it can no longer be considered patriotic to invest in them. They are losers. The government has made it very convenient to purchase savings bonds on a weekly basis. Many large corporations allow wage-earners to have a portion of their paychecks withheld to buy savings bonds. Minimum issue price is only $25 per bond. The interest is tax-deferred until maturity. The real travesty is that Series E bonds return only 6-7 percent interest at maturity. Imagine accumulating Series E bonds for 10 years in the face of double-digit inflation—by the end of 10 years, your purchasing power has decreased until you are worse off than if you had *spent* the money!

● *Company matching savings programs* can be great—or they can be a waste. Typically the company agrees to match an amount of money for every $1 you buy of company stock, up to certain limitations. If the company's stock performs well, this is an excellent way to invest. But, quite frequently, the company's stock flounders in a bear market along with other blue-chip stocks. Before signing up for such a program you should investigate it from an investment point of view, and not do it simply because the company will match your investment.

● *Single-premium deferred annuities* offer some good features, notably tax deferral and high interest. They also discourage impulsive withdrawal with a 5 percent penalty. But, again, the return simply does not match the inflation raging in this country. Most have been yielding about 10 percent during the past year. (However, don't confuse single-premium annuities with "variable" annuities, which I *do* recommend because of their potential to beat inflation. I cover this in chapter 11 on tax shelters).

Investments to Consider

So what *can* you do to stay ahead of inflation? In the remaining pages of this book, I'll tell you all about some tremendous inflation hedges where you can finally put your savings to work for rapid appreciation over the next several years. Such investments include:

- Gold and silver U. S. coins
- No-load mutual funds with excellent performance during bull *and* bear markets
- Hard foreign currencies, such as the Swiss franc and German mark
- Your own home, income-producing properties, and other lucrative real estate deals
- Tax shelters in oil & gas developments and other natural resources that promise high profit potential
- Stamps, gems, rare coins, art and other collectibles

Moreover, I'll show you some simple techniques for knowing *when to switch* between a variety of investments for maximum profits. Once you've obtained such profits, I'll show you ways to legally eliminate or defer paying taxes. These may seem like areas for the sophisticated investor alone, but this is all written with a low budget in mind.

Welcome to the world of high finance!

CHAPTER 3

YOUR HIGH-YIELDING SAVINGS ACCOUNT

"There are three faithful friends—
an old wife, an old dog, and ready money."

While the real profits to be made today are in the fields of stocks, precious metals, real estate, and other long-term investments, you still need a place to put your short-term cash. We talked in the previous chapter about the need for a short-term savings plan, to be drawn on when unexpected expenses come up. We also discussed the need for a place to "park" your long-term savings or investment funds from time to time, while waiting for changes in the investment outlook. Ideally you should have two separate accounts for these two purposes, so that the funds do not mix. But where should you place these short-term savings for maximum liquidity and maximum yield?

Upper-income investors seldom if ever park their idle funds in a passbook savings account paying a paltry 6 percent. They can take advantage of the superior yields available on large ($100,000) bank certificates of deposit, which yield double-digit rates. Or they place their funds in Treasury bills, which have returned anywhere from 7 to 16 percent recently. Minimum purchase, $10,000. Other possibilities include such esoteric vehicles as banker's acceptances, commercial paper, Eurodollar deposits, or other highly liquid money market certificates. But in every case, the minimum investment requires thousands of dollars, far beyond the pocketbook of any small investor.

The Money Funds

Now, fortunately, there are a few reliable low-cost sources for the small investor to earn high returns on his short-term savings and investment funds that are temporarily idle. You have probably heard of *money market funds*. These are mutual funds that pool the resources of thousands of investors to take advantage of high yields on Treasury bills, large bank CDs, commercial paper, etc. This way the high minimum requirements can be spread out among a number of smaller investors, so that you don't have to have $10,000 or more to get started.

The advantages of money market funds are:

● *High yields.* Money funds earned nearly 17 percent in early 1980 during the credit squeeze, and as low as 5 percent in 1976. But they will almost always give a better return than the passbook rate at savings institutions.

● *"No load," or no commissions.* You don't have to pay a broker a commission to buy into the money fund. One hundred percent of your money goes to work earning high returns, right away.

● *Minimum investment is low.* You don't have to have a small fortune to invest—most funds require just $1,000, and two funds require *no* minimum!

● *No penalty for withdrawal.* You don't have to wait until maturity to collect on the money fund investments. Just write a check.

● *Check-writing privilege.* Withdrawing your money is simple, using the free checks the fund sends you with which to redeem your "shares." Thus, money funds are like interest-bearing checking accounts. Most funds require you to write a check for at least $500, but we'll give you the names and addresses of a select few that have smaller minimums, as low as $250.

● *Easy to follow and convenient.* Most funds offer a toll-free 800 number to call for information, or to open an account. You can also track the weekly return on all funds in Monday's *Wall Street Journal.*

Recommended Money Funds

I would recommend the following funds for their low minimums, stability, and good service:

Name of Money Fund and address	Phone Number	Minimum	Recent Rate of return	Minimum Check-writing
American Liquid Trust 99 High St. Boston, MA 02104	800-225-2618 617-338-3300	None	11.32	$500
Alliance Capital Reserves, Inc. 120 Broadway New York, NY 10271	800-221-5672 212-635-3407	None	11.71	$500
Midwest Income Investment Co. 508 Dixie Terminal Cincinnati, OH 45202	800-543-0407 513-579-0414	$500	10.47	$350
NEL Cash Management Account 501 Boylston St. Boston, MA 02117	800-225-7670 617-267-6600	$1,000	10.66	$250
Money Market, Management 421 Seventh Ave. Pittsburgh, PA 15219	800-245-2423 412-288-1948	$1,000	9.76	$250
First Variable Rate Fund 1700 Pennsylvania Ave. NW Washington, DC 20006	800-424-2444 202-328-4010	$2,000	11.49	$500

Capital Preservation Fund 755 Page Mill Palo Alto, CA 94304	800-227-8380 800-982-5873 (CA) 415-858-2400	$1,000	10.77	$500
Kemper Money Market Fund, Inc. 120 South LaSalle St. Chicago, IL 60603	800-621-1048 312-346-3223	$1,000	12.15	$500
Union Cash Management Fund, Inc. One Bankers Trust Plaza New York, NY 10006	800-221-2450 212-432-4000	$1,000	12.08	$500

The yields differ from one money fund to another because each fund invests in a different variety of money market instruments. Recently, for example, American Liquid Trust was invested in mostly banker's acceptances. Midwest was into U. S. debt obligations repurchase agreements. NEL was divided into commercial paper and banker's acceptances. Capital Preservation Fund is virtually always 100 percent invested in Treasury bills, thus being the safest of all funds.

Clearly the investor with little funds should consider either American Liquid Trust or Alliance Capital Reserves to begin his savings program—the minimum investment is zero! Midwest Income is a close second, with a $500 minimum, and check-writing minimum of $350. NEL and Money Market both offer the lowest check-writing minimum of $250, but the minimum investment is $1,000 to open an account.

CHAPTER 4

THE SMALL INVESTOR'S GOLD MINE

"Genius without education is like silver in the mine."

Throughout history, gold has been universally recognized as a measure of money. Battles have been fought over it, the Americas were settled in search of it, and as long as the dollar was tied to it we had a fairly stable economy.

Gold and silver are the first lines of defense, protecting you from government-created inflation and economic or political crises. They belong in everyone's portfolio. Thus, the precious metals will be discussed here as your first high-powered investment and an excellent inflation hedge.

Wealthy Europeans, Asians, and now Americans have recognized the value of holding gold bullion, coins, and gold shares. An ounce of gold bullion sold for $35 in 1970. Today it sells for over $600! No government savings bond, no whole life cash value insurance, no annuity, and no savings account comes anywhere near a 2000 percent increase in 10 years! In fact, gold was ranked as the number one inflation hedge for the decade of the 1970s by Salomon Brothers, a Wall Street investment firm. You might be interested in their ranking of common investments during 1970-80:

RANKING OF INVESTMENTS

Investment	Average Annual Return 1970-1980	Investment	Average Annual Return 1970-1980
Gold	31.6%	Old Masters	13.4%
Oil	31.6%	U. S. Farmland	12.6%
Silver	23.7%	Housing	10.2%
U. S. Stamps	21.6%	Consumer Price Index	7.7%
Chinese ceramics	18.8%	Foreign Currencies	7.5%
Rare books	16.1%	Stocks	6.8%
U. S. coins	16.0%	Bonds	6.4%
Diamonds	15.1%		

The following graph should give you a pretty good indication of how gold has appreciated during the past decade.

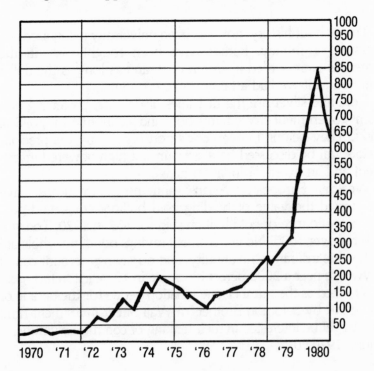

Note that gold didn't increase steadily in a straight line, but moved up in cyclical fashion. It tended to move up sharply when inflation accelerated, but dropped off when inflation subsided. During the 1970s, when inflation rates were generally moving up, the price of gold followed suit. It was the perfect inflation hedge.

One fundamental fact you must learn to live with if you are going to beat inflation is that you have to expect the prices of your inflation hedges to move up *and* down. You can't depend on a steady, guaranteed appreciation, unless you are willing to settle for the low returns of a savings account. In the *short run,* you can lose some of your principal when you invest in gold and other inflation hedges, and you must learn to live with the fact that the price of gold can drop for a period of time before it moves up. For instance, if you had bought gold in January, 1975—when it became legal for Americans to own gold bullion again—you would have paid about $200 an ounce. By August, 1976, the price of gold had dropped to $110 an ounce and, on paper, you would have lost nearly half your investment!

But if you had had the stamina to hold on for the long term, your $200 investment would look pretty good today—now that gold is selling for nearly $700 an ounce!

If you can live with that kind of price gyration, and if you can become astute at selecting the best long-term investments, you will soon be way ahead of the game.

Buying Gold Bullion

At $35 an ounce, gold bullion bars were a feasible investment vehicle. But at today's prices a standard 400-ounce bar would sell for nearly $300,000! Even a 32-ounce, one-kilo bar would cost over $20,000. So bullion bars have truly become an investment available only to the super-rich.

Of course, gold bullion bars are available in other sizes, commonly 100 ounces, 10 ounces, 5 ounces, and even 1 ounce. They are sold by major refiners and banks, such as Swiss Credit Bank, Deak-Perera Group, Englehart, Bank of Nova Scotia, and others.

A small investor could purchase a 1 ounce gold bullion bar for about 10 percent premium over the actual price, but I don't recommend it. Bullion bars are often hard to sell back to a bank or dealer. Often an assaying fee is required, to determine the genuine content of the bar. In addition, bullion bars aren't as convenient as bullion coins, such as the Krugerrand or Canadian Maple Leaf, for trading purposes. My advice is that you never take possession of bullion bars, except if you wish to display them on your desk!

Gold bullion is worth purchasing, however. If you view it purely as an *investment*, to be held by a reputable bank or gold dealer, it is an excellent, convenient way to invest in gold without the hassles of taking actual possession of it. Transactions can be negotiated instantly, often by phone, and sometimes even faster than buying or selling coins.

During the frenzied bull market in gold during 1979-80, many coin dealers and banks refused to give quotes over the phone or over the counter. You couldn't buy and you couldn't sell your gold or silver *coins* for a period of time because of the volatility of prices. But if you had bought gold *bullion* and had it held for you by Citibank, Merrill Lynch, or Swiss Credit Bank, you could still have sold that gold instantly, based on the London price-fix for gold on that particular day. So sometimes it does pay to own gold bullion for complete liquidity.

Inexpensive, Low-Priced Gold Bullion

Now at last you can buy gold bullion in very small amounts. In fact, you can even purchase less than an ounce of bullion now, so don't let that $700 price scare you off.

Merrill Lynch has come to the rescue of the novice investor

with an innovative way to buy gold bullion for as little as $100! It's called Merrill Lynch's Gold Sharebuilders Plan.

Minimum investment is only $100—a fantastic deal for small investors. You can add to your account afterwards with as little as $50. Purchases will be figured to four decimal places, such as 0.5435 ounces. Each day, Merrill Lynch combines all its orders from shareholders and then buys in bulk at $1 over the London afternoon price fix. The commissions are higher for smaller purchasers, however. The commission for a $100 purchase is 5½ percent, while the fee schedule drops to 1½ percent at the $5,000 level.

Another great advantage is that there are no storage or insurance fees! (Most gold plans charge an annual fee of ½ percent.) You also avoid sales tax when you buy, and assaying charges when you sell. Merrill Lynch will send you a quarterly statement. This is clearly the best gold purchasing plan to come on the market today for the small investor. For a free brochure on the plan, write:

> Merrill Lynch Gold Sharebuilders Plan
> Merrill Lynch, Inc.
> One Liberty Plaza
> New York, NY 10080
> Toll-free 800-221-2856
> or in New York, 800-522-8882

Or contact your local Merrill Lynch office.

Other Gold Plans

You may also wish to investigate the gold programs of other banks and coin dealers.

Citibank offers a gold certificate program with a $1,000 minimum. A certificate represents a specified amount of ownership in gold bullion. Commissions are 3 percent to buy, and 1 percent to sell, and there's a ½ percent storage fee *after* the first year. The gold price is based on the New York Commodity exchange quotes. The bullion is stored for you in your choice of three locations—London, Zurich or Delaware. For a brochure and further information, write:

Citibank Gold Purchase Plan
Citibank Gold Center
399 Park Ave.
New York, NY 10043
Toll-free 800-223-1080
or in New York, 212-559-6041

Deak & Co. (Washington) was one of the first gold dealers to offer a gold certificate program. Minimum investment is $2,500, commissions are 3 percent to buy, 1 percent to sell, plus an annual storage fee of ½ percent at the start of the second year. For details, write:

Deak's Gold Certificate Program
Deak & Co. (Washington)
1800 K St. NW
Washington, D. C. 20006
Toll-free 800-424-1186
Or in Washington, D. C., 202-872-1233

Deak's certificate program also includes a great variety of other precious metals and coins—including silver bullion, platinum, palladium, silver dimes, quarters, half-dollars, or dollars, and gold Krugerrands, Maple Leafs, Mexican 50 Pesos, Coronas, and British Sovereigns.

Low Cost Gold Coins

The most popular large gold coins are the Krugerrand (1 troy ounce gold), the Canadian Maple Leaf (1 ounce), the Austrian and Hungarian 100 Coronas (.9802 ounce), and the Mexican 50 Peso (1.2056 ounce). At the current gold price of nearly $700 an ounce, these coins are selling at from $700 to $850 a piece. As you can see, the larger gold coins have all reached astronomical values as gold has climbed to unbelievable heights.

So it's quite understandable that many smaller investors are searching for smaller coins. The following is a list of smaller gold coins, their fineness, and their pure gold content:

Smaller Gold Coins

Type of Coin	Fineness	Pure Gold Content (troy oz.)
Austrian 4 Ducat	.986	.4438
British Sovereign	.917	.2354
Mexican 20 Peso	.900	.4823
Mexican 10 Peso	.900	.24113
Mexican 5 Peso	.900	.12057
Mexican 2½ Peso	.900	.06028
Mexican 2 Peso	.900	.04822
S. African ½ Rand	.917	.5000
S. African ¼ Rand	.917	.2500
S. African ⅒ Rand	.917	.1000

These are all bullion-type coins, i.e., they are priced mainly for their gold content rather than for their numismatic value. The British Sovereign is considered a semi-rare coin, and thus carries a larger premium than the other coins (often over 20 percent). In every case, the premium or commission on the smaller coins will be higher than that charged for the larger, 1 ounce gold coins. Nevertheless, even at today's high gold prices, you can still buy the smallest gold coin, the Mexican 2 peso, for $40 or so.

Recently South Africa's Chamber of Mines began issuing 4 different sizes of Krugerrands: 1 ounce, ½ ounce, ¼ ounce, and ⅒ ounce coins. Commissions increase substantially the smaller

Comparison

the coin. A recent survey showed that the 1 oz. Krugerrand had a 6.2 percent commission, ½ oz. a 10.6 percent commission, ¼ oz. a 10.6 percent commission, and $\frac{1}{10}$ oz. a huge 20.1 percent commission. Frankly, I think buying gold bullion from Merrill Lynch's Gold Sharebuilders Plan would be better, where the commission on $100 worth of bullion is 5½ percent.

U. S. Common-Dated Gold Coins

The U. S. Treasury discontinued minting U. S. gold coins in 1933, and has not minted any gold coins since. It is currently producing 1-oz. and ½-oz. "medallions," but it is still uncertain whether they will find a liquid market among coin dealers.

U. S. gold coins—such as the $20 double eagle, the $10 eagle, and the $5 half-eagle—are all sold at considerable premiums over gold bullion value because of their rarity. The common-dated U. S. gold coins have premiums as low as 30 percent, even in "brilliant uncirculated" condition. The market is very liquid in these common-dated eagles, and they should definitely be included as part of your coin portfolio.

Silver Coins: Poor Man's Gold?

Silver has traditionally sold for considerably less than the yellow metal, and is often called the poor man's gold. However, its rate of appreciation has been almost as rapid and therefore is an excellent inflation hedge. In 1970, silver bullion sold for around $1.65 an ounce. By 1980, it had reached a new high of nearly $50 an ounce, although it has since then fallen to the $15-20 range. The following chart shows the change in the price of silver from 1970.

Index — *Silver Inflation* — $/oz.

23.7 compounded annual return

Salomon Brothers ranked silver as the number-three inflation hedge during the 1970s, with a 23.7 percent compounded annual return.

Silver coins are the best medium for small investors who want to get into precious metals. U. S. silver dimes, quarters, half-dollars, and dollars that were minted prior to 1965 are often referred to as "junk" silver—but this junk is a real treasure. By 1965 the value of the silver used in minting coins exceeded the face value of the coins, and consequently they became collector's items. Today a silver dime sells for around $1.50—so you can see how silver coins are a valuable investment tool for the person just starting out.

The following chart shows the pure silver content of silver coins (all U. S. coins contained 90 percent silver).

U. S. Silver Coins

Type of Coins	*Pure Silver Content (troy ounces)*
Dimes, 1916-64	.07234 oz,
Quarters, 1916-64	.18084 oz.
Half-dollars, 1916-64	.36169 oz.
Kennedy 40% silver Half-dollars, 1965-70	.14792 oz.
Peace & Morgan Dollars 1878-1935	.77344 oz.
Eisenhower 40% Silver Dollars, 1971-76 (Proof only)	.31625 oz.

The small investor's best bet is to buy "junk" silver dimes, quarters, half dollars, or dollars. I would avoid the Kennedy and Eisenhower 40-percent coins which were minted from 1965-70, except as a novelty. If you're buying for silver content only, not for the beauty or rarity of the coin, "junk" silver offers you the lowest premium.

Silver coins can be bought in any quantity. The most expensive, but the best value, are called *"bags"* because you receive a bag of coins whose face value totals $1,000. You can purchase half-bags, ($500 face value) quarter-bags, ($250 face value) or tenth-bags, ($100 face value). Expect to pay about 15 times the face value at current prices ($15-$20 an ounce).

Rolls of coins can fit more easily into the small investor's portfolio. Dimes come in rolls of 50 with a face value of $5, while quarters are packaged 40 to a roll and have a $10 face value. The wrappers look just like those that are used by the bank today. So be sure you don't accidentally use them for doing the laundry!

Individual coins can also be purchased. A silver dime sells today for about $1.50—*anyone* can become a hard-money investor at that price!

Where to Buy at the Lowest Price

The markets for gold and silver coins are not as precise as the New York stock exchange, and prices vary considerably among coin dealers. During the recent turmoil in the silver market, $1,000-face value "junk" bags varied in price by as much as $2,000! It pays to shop around, especially when the markets become volatile.

One of the best coin dealers I've found for the small purchaser is:

> Auric United Corporation
> 15748 Interstate Highway
> University National Bank Building
> P. O. Box 29467
> San Antonio, TX 78229
> Toll-free 800-531-5777
> or in Texas, 512-696-1234 (collect)

Auric United Corporation is an affiliate of United Services Fund, a no-load mutual fund specializing in gold shares. A.U. Corp. deals in all the small coins mentioned earlier, as well as the larger, more popular, coins. A. U. Corp.'s motto is "no order is too small." The price you pay for the small coins is the wholesale cost (the cost A. U. Corp. actually pays in the New York market) plus a small fee for handling, shipping and insurance charges.

At the present time, handling charges are as follows:

—$6 per coin plus $5 shipping for lots of 1 to 19 coins.

—$3 per coin plus $10 shipping for lots of 20 to 99 coins.

—$2 per coin and *no* shipping charge for lots of 100 or more.

Charges are slightly higher for larger coins. For Krugerrands, currently selling for $700 a piece, the markup on a single coin is $10 plus $6 for shipping.

A. U. Corp. has developed several innovative programs for the small purchaser, such as their coin(s)-of-the-month program. Under this plan, A. U. Corp. will purchase a certain number of coins on your behalf at the beginning of each month, and bill you for the coin(s). The coins will be shipped to you, or you can have them held for future delivery.

This kind of automatic monthly purchase would fit well into your "savings first" plan, as we discussed in the chapter on budgeting. It's also a very good way to average the cost of your coin purchases, since prices will fluctuate during their long-term rise.

A. U. Corp. has a similar "roll(s)-a-month" program for the automatic purchase of rolls of silver dollars, halves, quarters or dimes.

Charges on silver coin purchases at A. U. Corp. are set as follows:

—1000 silver dollars, cost plus $150 plus $65 shipping.
—Roll of 20 silver dollars, cost plus $15 plus $5 shipping.
—$1,000 face value bag, cost plus $100 plus $65 shipping.
—Roll of 20 halves, 40 quarters, or 50 dimes, cost plus $10 plus $5 shipping.

There are, of course, many other coin dealers that offer a similar monthly coin purchase plan. But I was impressed with the pricing system of Auric United.

Don't take my word for it however. Prices and programs do change, so shop around. Below are the toll-free 800 numbers of several major coin dealers where you can have gold and silver coins sent to you by mail. Get a quote from each of them on the coins you wish to buy. Be sure to call all of them at about the same time, since prices vary during the day. And be sure to ask for the full *delivered* price.

Numisco (Chicago)	Monex (Los Angeles)
800-621-5272	800-854-3361
	800-432-7013 (Calif.)
Blanchard & Co.	Deak & Co.
(New Orleans)	(Washington, D. C.)
800-535-8588	800-424-1186
Investment Rarities	Bramble Coins
(Minneapolis)	(Michigan)
800-328-2860	800-248-5952

Like gold bullion, bars of silver bullion can be purchased from major coin dealers and banks. Again, I don't recommend taking delivery of the bars—they should be held by the bank and used exclusively for trading or as a convenient way to hold silver for the long term. Steer clear of silver bars sold by little-known or brand-new companies or "refiners." In the early 1970s, several silver firms went bankrupt, and customers were often charged assaying fees and were paid below-market prices when they tried to sell.

Avoid the Sales Tax

Most states impose a sales tax on the purchase of gold and silver bullion and coins. To avoid that additional expense, it's best to buy through the mail from out-of-state dealers. Legally you're not required to pay a sales tax if you buy coins from a company located in another state. The firms listed above are all reputable.

If you wish to buy in person without paying a sales tax, you can usually buy tax-free at a *coin show*. Coin shows are held every couple of months in major cities around the country—call your local coin dealer for the next show in your area. It's a great learning experience. All kinds of bullion and rare coins are on display, as well as medallions, stamps, and other pieces of art. You can buy and sell anonymously, or if you prefer, you can use your checkbook. Dealer-to-dealer trades are not subject to a sales tax. Most coin dealers at the show consider customers to be fellow coin dealers, not retail customers. But beware—you'll be tempted to buy everything under the sun when you see all the glittering beauty at the show.

How to Buy Gold Stocks

Wealthy investors have long known that gold shares, or buying stock in an actual mine, can offer the opportunity for highly-leveraged gains while paying superior dividends at the same time. Gold shares have always been regarded as speculative, however, requiring the investor to have sufficient assets to cover the substantial risks. Thus, gold shares have traditionally been a rich man's investment, a vehicle known for its lucrative gains—or its high losses. Stockbrokers will tell you that in order to minimize the risks involved, you should diversify by investing in a variety of gold shares, not just one or two favorites. One may plunge, and another skyrocket, with others performing somewhere in between. This way, you don't have to gamble on finding the one that skyrockets. T.E. Slanker Co., a New York brokerage firm specializing in gold shares, insists that you invest at least $20,000 in order to diversify properly. Since few stockbrokers are gold share experts, the shrewd investor must turn to specialists like Slanker, who charges full standard commissions, averaging 5 percent per trade. This can become quite expensive, especially for the novice.

Fortunately, there is a unique alternative for the small investor. The simple, yet often overlooked way, is through purchasing shares of a *mutual fund*. Buying through a fund allows you to pool your money with other investors. It offers wide diversification, professional management, convenience, and small transaction costs. In fact, two mutual funds I recommend charge no sales commission at all! They are called no-load mutual funds.

The First recommended fund is:

United Services Fund
15748 Interstate Highway
P.O. Box 29467
San Antonio, TX 78229
Toll-free 800-531-5777
or in Texas, 512-696-1234

United Services Fund, as mentioned earlier, is the parent company of Auric United Corporation, the coin dealer. United Services invests mostly in South African mining shares, and pays a decent dividend as well (recently as high as 10 percent). About 15 percent is invested in North American mining shares. Despite the political and economic risks associated with investing in South African golds, USF has been the number-one performing mutual fund in the U.S. for the past two years. It gained 135 percent in the past year, so you can see that the potential for profit justifies the risk. Annual expenses have been held to a minimum—about 1 percent, which is superior compared to many mutual funds. Minimum investment is only $500.

Golconda Investors, Ltd., the second recommended no load gold mutual fund, offers some alternatives to USF. Golconda managers attempt to "trade" the gold market, while USF tends to "buy and hold" gold shares. Consequently you are more dependent on astute management to perform well. As a result, trading costs and administrative fees are higher—an average 5 percent for the past year. The fund is also heavily into gold bullion at the present, while holding only a few dozen South African gold shares. Thus, Golconda should be regarded as more speculative than USF. Golconda's performance did not match USF in the past few years, but the return was still a remarkable 112 percent in 1979. Minimum investment is also only $500.

Golconda has recently added a new feature—a telephone-switch privilege for its customers. Golconda is a member of a group of funds, called "Bull and Bear Funds," which invest in a variety of securities. It's now possible for customers who perceive that gold is about to drop to switch by telephone out of Golconda and into an affiliated money-market fund, Dollar Reserves, to preserve their capital during a bear market in gold.

For details and a prospectus, write or call:

Golconda Investors Ltd.
111 Broadway
New York, NY 10006
Toll-free 800-523-9250
Or, in New York, 212 267-5100

At the present time, USF and Golconda are only marginally invested in North American mining companies, which tend to pay smaller dividends than their South African counterparts. However, if political troubles appear to present a serious danger to the value of the South African gold shares, either fund can dispose of its African holdings and buy North American stocks. This is the kind of flexibility available in a managed fund. It pays to watch the portfolio mix of the funds in which you invest.

Summary on Gold and Silver

In conclusion, I have found that the small investor can profit from a portfolio in gold and silver bullion, coins and shares. He can do it conveniently, safely, at low cost, and with little risk. He can buy bullion with as little as $100, have it stored free outside the country, and avoid expensive fees. He can buy a single gold coin, a roll of silver dimes, or higher priced coins from reputable dealers at a low premium and without paying a sales tax. He can even speculate in exotic gold mining shares, with only $500 and without paying sales commission. The rich aren't so different, after all!

CHAPTER 5

LOW-RISK, LOW-COST INVESTING IN THE STOCK MARKET

"No gains without pains."

Contrary to what you may have heard or read, the stock market is very much alive and well in the financial world. The 30 industrial stocks that make up the Dow Jones Industrial Average have gone through some rough times in the past 15 years, victims of high inflation and onerous taxation. But the stock market is much bigger than the 30 industrials. Thousands of companies of every size are traded on the New York Stock Exchange, the American Stock Exchange and Over the Counter. The stock market is still undoubtedly the most liquid trading market in the world of finance.

Savvy professionals have continued to make spectacular gains by choosing their stocks carefully. The "buy and hold" strategy that made your grandfather's fortune simply doesn't work for most stocks any longer. Insiders on Wall Street have learned to switch from one stock to another for maximum profits. They have even learned how to profit when stocks drop, through the put-and-call option market. Sophisticated money managers utilize such exotic vehicles as warrants, preferred stock, convertible bonds, naked calls—all in an effort to make big money for their customers. Others have taken advantage of tremendous bull markets in foreign stock exchanges—those in London, Zurich, Mexico City, Singapore, Toronto, and Tokyo.

Yes, wealthy investors and people-in-the-know have been able to take full advantage of these opportunities. They have the money it takes to have new investment opportunities in the U. S. and around the world investigated by Wall Street money managers. They can afford to pay the high fees, and to put up the million-dollar minimum investment requirements.

But there is room on Wall Street for the small investor, too.

The Problem With Stockbrokers

Typically, the small investor has little alternative but to turn to the local stockbroker in his home town. Since he's had little experience in the world of investments, he relies on the advice and tips of the broker. The neophyte customer may have only a few thousand dollars to invest, and the broker will recommend one or two issues "just to get started."

This is, in most cases, a fatal mistake for the novice investor! Most stockbrokers have no business investing a customer's hard-earned cash, albeit small, in one or two stocks. The cardinal principle of any broker worth his salt should be diversification to spread risk!

As a financial consultant, I deal with hundreds of small investors who have made the mistake of investing a little money in a couple of stocks. Most of the time, I've never heard of the stocks they bought. "Where in the world did you learn about these issues?" I ask. Invariably the answer is, "From my stockbroker." And, more times than not, the stocks have dropped in value!

Another major problem with dealing with a "full service" broker is that he is often unwilling to carry out your wishes. When you want to buy a particular stock or stock industry, you often may have to argue with him. He may try to talk you into one of his pet stocks. Most new investors don't know enough to fight back, and end up going along with the broker. Then, if the recommended stocks drop in value and you want to sell, frequently the broker again argues against it, convincing you to "hold on" for a turnaround.

I'm not condemning all "full service" stockbrokers. Many customers have developed an excellent, fruitful relationship with their brokers. Many brokers are honest, forthright, and most importantly, accurate advisors. But my experience has been that these gems are few and far between. The prudent investor, who is just starting out in the investment world, would be wise to avoid them for now.

Discount Brokers

One alternative would be the use of a discount broker. These brokers take your order rather than give advice, and charge a lower commission. Discount brokers have reduced their commissions by up to 70 percent of the standard NYSE rate. So if you want to trade stocks and bonds, this is the low cost way to do it. And, since most have toll-free numbers, you can easily deal with a discount broker from another state. You don't have to deal with a local stockbroker unless you want to.

If you go this route, you must know what you're doing. As your own money manager, you must know which stocks to select, how long to hold them, and when to switch. If you hesitate to be your own investment manager, consider a recent study comparing individual traders with professional money managers. The study was conducted by three business school professors who examined the results of 2,500 individual stock-trading accounts. Their conclusion was: "Individuals turned out to be surprisingly skillful investors. . . The argument that professionals do better at selecting stocks than 'the little guy' doesn't hold up. The common belief that professionals get superior results is just investment community folklore."

The performance of discount brokers has been mixed. Some have had serious problems with executing the wrong orders, overcharging, or not recognizing certain classes of stock. I once called a discount broker, and gave him a list of several gold stocks to purchase. Although all were listed under "foreign securities" in the *Wall Street Journal*, the clerk had difficulty locating several of them on the exchanges. You need to be very careful in choosing a discount broker.

Major discounters advertise in the financial newspapers such as the *Wall Street Journal* and *Barron's*. They usually offer toll-free 800 numbers.

Here is a list of discount brokers who have recently advertised their services nationally.

	Toll-free Number	*Minimum Commission*
Marquette de Bary Co. 30 Broad St. New York, NY 10004	800-221-3305	$20
StockCross, Inc. 1 Washington Mall Boston, MA 02108	800-225-6196	$25+
Quick & Reilly, Inc. 120 Wall St. New York, NY 10005	800-221-5220	$30
Fidelity Brokerage Services, Inc. P. O. Box 2698 201 Devonshire St., 2nd Floor Boston, MA 02208	800-225-2097	$20+
Charles Schwab & Co. One Second St. San Francisco, CA 94105	800-648-5311	$24

High Performance Mutual Funds

If you lack the confidence or skill to trade the stock market yourself, perhaps a better solution for the neophyte investor would again be the purchase of mutual funds, this time one that invests in the stock market.

Mutual funds enjoyed a fine reputation during the 1950s and early 1960s, but in the late 1960s many of them collapsed.

The Penny Capitalist warns the small investor: ". . . the funds have out-performed the averages on an up market, but have sunk more rapidly than the averages in a down market. . . On balance, the averages have out-performed the funds."

While the writer makes a valid point, he fails to consider the fact that a *few* funds have continued to make spectacular profits throughout the past 15-year period, through both bear and bull markets. Moreover, it is now possible to switch out of a mutual fund and into a more profitable fund or alternative investment, *without* paying any penalty or commissions. It is plain to see that by choosing a well-managed fund you can still make a good profit in the stock market, without having to constantly monitor your portfolio.

Commission or No Commission?

There are two kinds of mutual funds—no-load, and load. Load funds require the investor to pay 4-8 percent to the broker up front when he invests. No-load funds require no commissions at all—they are sold directly by the management company without the use of brokers, so 100 percent of your money goes to work.

Which is better? Clearly for the small investor, the no-loads win.

With a load fund, the price has to rise by 4-8 percent just to break even. This not only becomes expensive but begins to cloud your judgment as well, since there is a tendency to stay with the investment "until I earn my money back." It inhibits trading, and in this ever-changing economy you have to be willing to trade.

More importantly, studies have shown that load funds do not outperform the no-load funds. The most recent survey of mutual funds by *Forbes* concluded: "Year after year, the *Forbes* survey has found no basis for thinking load funds do better than no-loads, or vice versa. This year as last, one-third of the funds that made *Forbes'* honor roll were no-loads."

The no-load market is booming, and 25 percent of all mutual funds are now no-loads. The advantages are outstanding.

Advantages of No-Load Mutual Funds

First, no sales commissions. A full 100 percent of your money is placed in the fund. You could conceivably buy one day and sell the next, without any penalties or commissions. Any costs or administrative fees are spread out over the year, and are figured into the value of the shares. Annual expenses are important and should be watched carefully when you invest. *Forbes* magazine does an annual survey of costs and performance of mutual funds each September. You would be wise to purchase a copy.

Second, no broker. You completely avoid the pushy broker. It's up to you how you invest, where you invest, and when you invest. You call the mutual fund, they don't call you. Your other investments are strictly your own business. And since you don't have to fill out any revealing customer forms, as brokerage firms require, you have a good deal of privacy.

Third, diversification. The mutual fund invests in a large variety of companies. Even if the fund specializes in a particular industrial group, the fund is large enough to buy dozens of companies, thus spreading the risk.

Fourth, professional management. You get the professional management that was formerly available only to wealthy investors. When you pool your financial resources with thousands of other investors, you can afford money managers who work fulltime investing on your behalf. The management varies considerably from fund to fund, and from time to time, so this is by far the most important item to monitor when investing in mutual funds.

Fifth, convenience. Many no-load mutual funds offer toll-free 800 numbers to answer inquiries, and even permit buying and selling by phone! The telephone-switch privilege allows you to switch out of a no-load fund when you think it's going to fall, and into a safe and secure money market fund immediately. Conversely, when you foresee a market rally you can buy into the mutual fund as fast as a phone call.

The "net asset value" (the price at which you can buy or sell the fund) is set every day, and published in most major newspapers around the country, as well as in the *Wall Street Journal.* They are listed under "Mutual Funds" or "Investment Funds." So it's simple to find out how your fund is doing. And with no sales commission, you don't have to deduct any sales charges when figuring your performance.

Finally, one mutual fund is a lot easier to buy and sell than a large list of stocks. When you decide to sell, you don't have to consider the merits of each individual stock, wondering if you should hang onto some and sell others. You simply sell the mutual fund.

Sixth, liquidity. You can buy or sell at any time, without penalty. You can redeem your shares by writing a letter, or by calling the fund on the phone. Many funds permit withdrawal by telephone, bank wire (money is wired directly to your bank account), or by check.

Seventh, tax advantages. Mutual funds have the same tax advantages of individual stocks. If you hold them for more than a year, they qualify as long-term capital gains, making profits 60 percent tax-free. Mutual funds also qualify for Keogh, Individual Retirement Accounts, and corporate pension plans.

Great Variety

No-loads offer funds in virtually any category you may desire. There are over 280 no-loads on the market today. Most of them fit into one of these categories:

● Growth stocks (emphasize price appreciation, pay little or no dividend)

● Income funds (seek high dividends or interest from stocks, bonds, money market instruments. Good for those who need regular income from their investment.)

● Money market funds (high yield, check-writing privilege)

● Natural resource and energy funds

● International funds (invest in foreign securities)

● Municipal bond funds (tax-free yields, check-writing privilege)

● Gold share funds (invest in South African and North American mining shares)

● Government bond funds (safety, high yield)

● Corporate bond funds (higher yields, provide income)

● Specialty funds (embryonic companies, technology stocks, etc.)

How to Get Started

For a free list of no-load mutual funds, write:

> The Directory of No-Load Mutual Funds
> No-Load Mutual Fund Association, Inc.
> Valley Forge, PA 19481
> 215-783-7600

> Or: No-Load Mutual Funds Membership List
> Investment Company Institute
> 1775 K St. NW
> Washington, DC 20006
> 202-293-7700

Minimum investment requirements vary considerably. Most funds require a minimum of $500 to $3,000, with an average around $1,000.

For the absolutely rock-bottom stock market investor, there is good news. Now there is one management company fund that has *no* minimum investment, and better yet, it's on the *Forbes* honor roll! For a prospectus, write:

> 20th Century Select Investors
> 605 W. 47th St.
> Kansas City, MO 64112
> 816-531-5575

Twentieth Century Select Investors has a zero purchase requirement. This is ideal for someone just starting out, or for students, children, and others who have little money with which to begin. Performance has been excellent during the 1968-80 period, with a compounded annual rate of return of 11.0 percent. *Forbes* rated it "A" during bull markets and "A" during bear markets—one of only two no-loads so rated.

Twentieth Century Select pays some dividends, but it primarily seeks for capital appreciation. The fund was up 39.8 percent in the past year.

Other High Performance No-loads

Other no-load growth funds rated highly on the *Forbes* honor roll include:

Fund	Minimum Purchase	1968-80 Avg. Annual Return
Guardian Mutual Fund 522 Fifth Ave. New York, NY 10036 212-790-9800	$200	8.6%
Mutual Shares Corp. 170 Broadway New York, NY 10038 212-267-4200	$1,000	12.1%

Families of Funds

Many no-load mutual funds operate as a group, and are managed under a single investment group allowing you to switch between funds with ease. Some of these include:

The Vanguard Group

> Box 1100, Valley Forge, PA 19482, 800-523-7910, or 800-362-7688 in Pennsylvania only.
>
> Funds: Explorer, Municipal Bond Funds, High Yield Bond Fund, Windsor Fund, Whitehall Money Market Trust, etc.

Fidelity Group

> 82 Devonshire St., Boston, MA 02109, 800-225-6190, or 617-726-0650 in Mass.
>
> Funds: Contrafund, Asset Investment Trust, Fidelity Fund, Municipal Bond Fund, Aggressive Income, Cash Reserves, etc.

The Rowe Price Group

> 100 East Pratt St., Baltimore, MD 21202, 800-638-5660, 301-547-2308 in Maryland.
>
> Funds: New Income, New Era, New Horizons, Growth Stock, Prime Reserve, etc.

The Dreyfus Group

> 767 Fifth Ave., New York, NY 10022, 800-223-5525, or 212-935-5700 (in NY), 223-0303 (NY City collect), 935-6633 (NY State collect)
>
> Funds: A Bonds Plus, Special Income Fund, Dreyfus #9, Third Century Fund, Liquid Assets, Tax Exempt Bond Fund, etc.

The Scudder Group

> 345 Park Ave., New York, NY 10022, 800-225-2470, or 212-350-8200, 175 Federal St., Boston, MA 10110 (Main office)
>
> Funds: International Fund, Development Fund, Income Fund, Special Fund, Managed Municipal Bonds, Tax free Money Fund, Cash Management Trust, etc.

Of course there are other management groups which are listed in the newspaper under mutual funds. But these are the major ones.

Telephone Switch Privileges

A number of aggressive growth stock funds offer a telephone switch service for immediate buying and selling of fund shares. This has been available since 1975. As a shareholder, all you have to do is call the toll-free 800 number of the fund, and request that shares be transferred to the affiliated money market fund, or vice versa. Thus, everything can be done by phone at no charge to the customer; you have instant liquidity in the market; and most of the time, there's no charge for switching.

The stock market can be volatile, and prices of stocks can drop suddenly and drastically. Telephone switching can save you from the sudden bear markets. Some aggressive no-load growth funds have been known to lose 50 percent of their value in a bear market!

The following is a partial list of top-performing funds offering the telephone switch feature:

Mutual Fund	*Minimum Investment*	*Affiliated Money Market Fund*
Dreyfus Third Century or Dreyfus #9 767 Fifth Ave. New York, NY 10153 800-223-5525 212-935-5700 (in NY)	$500	Dreyfus Liquid Asset
Pennsylvania Mutual Fund 127 John St. New York, NY 10038 800-221-4268 212-269-8533 (in NY)	$500	Scudder Cash Investment Trust
Guardian Mutual Fund 522 Fifth Ave. New York, NY 10036 212-790-9800	$200	Daily Income Fund

Some specialized funds that offer telephone switch include:

Energy Fund 522 Fifth Ave. New York, NY 10036 212-790-9800	$100	Daily Income Fund
Scudder International Fund 345 Park Ave. New York, NY 10022 800-225-2470 212-350-8200	$1,000	Scudder Cash Investment Trust
Golconda Investors Ltd. (Gold Fund) 111 Broadway New York, NY 10006 800-523-9250 212-267-5100 (in NY)	$500	Dollar Reserves

How to Profit

To show you the advantages of switching within a family of funds, here is the true story of how a savvy investor recently profited from the variety of funds in the Fidelity group.

The customer began with $10,000 at the beginning of the year. He kept his money for the first 3½ months in the money market fund, Fidelity Cash Reserves, which at the time earned him between 13-14.5 percent interest, on an annualized basis. In March, interest rates finally started dropping, and he called Fidelity's toll-free number, transferring his money into Fidelity's Corporate Bond Fund. Within 6 weeks, the bond fund had appreciated 15 percent. In addition, he was earning about 11 percent interest, giving him a net worth in his account of $11,500. Finally, foreseeing the rise in the stock market, he switched into Fidelity's Asset Investment Trust, which in the next two months move up 19 percent! So, in less than 8 months, the customer had turned his $10,000 into $13,600—an annualized gain of approximately 50 percent.

If he had tried to trade the market in individual stocks and bonds, commissions would have cost him $400 to $500. But, by using a family fund, he didn't spend a dime on commissions —even the telephone calls were free!

We often think of millionaires sitting in their master suites making millions in the stock market with just a few phone calls. Well, now, the day of the armchair investor has arrived in middle America!

Simple Techniques for Trading

Trading can be a tricky business, however, and you can lose money if you aren't careful. Many investors, especially those just starting out, might not feel comfortable with it. If that's the case, stay with the proven performers, such as Twentieth

Century Select Investors, Guardian Mutual Fund, or Founders Special Fund. Even then you must be aware that no one can guarantee that future performance will be as good as the past. Management is prone to change attitudes and trading techniques from year to year. You must be willing to monitor the situation, and to switch to another fund if you don't like what you see.

If you are more adventuresome, and wish to avoid those "down" markets from time to time by switching between funds, there are some simple techniques you can use to help in your decision-making.

One has been developed by investment counselor Dick Fabian, who writes a monthly letter, called *Telephone Switch Newsletter*. His approach is totally "technical," meaning that he watches the funds' charts to determine whether they are a good buy at the time. He uses three technical indicators to decide whether to be into an equity mutual fund, for example, or to be in the money market fund for safety. Using this technique over the years, he has been able to profit from the bull markets in the mutual funds and to avoid the bear markets. During bull markets, he invests in equity growth funds. During bear markets, he keeps his money safe, in high-yielding money funds.

The technique is a simple one, but calculating the numbers can be a bit time-consuming. For those interested, I suggest you order his letter, *Telephone Switch Newsletter* (P. O. Box 2101, Huntington Beach, CA 92647, $85 a year). The price includes 12 issues, a 24-hour hot-line telephone service, and special bulletins, plus a copy of his book, *How to Be Your Own Investment Counselor— Through the Use of Telephone Switch Mutual Funds* ($15.95 normally).

Using the Discount Rate

The second approach is perhaps simpler, and all the information that is required can be found in the financial pages of your newspaper.

This technique hinges on the "discount rate." The discount rate is the interest the Federal Reserve charges its member banks for loans. It does not change as quickly as the corporate "prime rate" or other interest rates, so it is a powerful investment indicator. Whenever the discount rate is changed by the Federal Reserve, an announcement will be made in the *Wall Street Journal* or in the financial section of your local newspaper.

The key to profits is this:

—When the discount rate moves *down*, switch into growth mutual funds;

—When the discount rate moves *up*, switch into money market funds, *or* a gold mutual fund like United Services Fund or Golconda.

Why does this work? In the past, the stock market has performed best when interest rates have been stable or declining. But when interest rates start climbing, gold shares and money market funds have proven to be the better performers.

Harry Browne, who has developed this technique to the fullest, has shown the advantages of using the discount rate. The following chart compares the Dow Jones Industrial Average and the price of gold over the past 10 years.

Investment	Buy-Sell Dates	Compounded Annual Return
Gold	Jan., 1970-Nov. 1970	7.0%
Stocks	Nov., 1970-July, 1971	31.7%
Gold	July, 1971-Nov. 1971	32.1%
Stocks	Nov., 1971-Jan., 1973	32.9%
Gold	Jan. 1973-Dec., 1974	34.5%
Stocks	Dec., 1974-Aug., 1977	19.2%
Gold	Aug., 1977-May 1980	52.4%
Stocks	May, 1980-Sept. 1980	42.0%

As you can see from the above chart, switching between gold

and the stock market based on moves in the discount rate proved to be very profitable. You should be aware that gold and the stock market do not always move opposite each other nor will the move be immediate.(Note, for example, that the discount rate went up in September, 1980, but gold dropped!) This switching technique is therefore not meant to be a short-term trading system. Perhaps it would be best called a medium-term trading program.

Guide to Growth Stocks

If you invest in several mutual funds, you may want to track them in more detail. The best monthly service on mutual funds, with charts, commentaries, and additional market information, is

Growth Fund Guide
Growth Fund Research Bldg.
Eureka, CA 96097

Annual U. S. subscription is $58, but you can get a current issue by sending $2.

Your Trading Philosophy

In summary, your trading philosophy is very important when you invest in the stock market. You can be the speculative "hare" by moving in and out of no-load mutual funds for maximum profit. Or you can be the conservative "tortoise" who carefully selects mutual funds for long-term appreciation. In either case, the race is ultimately dependent upon the management of the funds, so it is crucial to monitor their performance.

Wall Street no longer needs to sound like an exotic, faraway land.

CHAPTER 6

WHERE TO EARN HIGH MONTHLY INCOME

*"He that is rich need not live sparingly,
and he that can live sparingly need not be rich."*

It is an obvious fact, but it bears repeating: Different investors have different financial goals. The investment needs of a couple in their thirties with three young children and little or no savings or equity will vary greatly from that of a retired widow with a paid-off mortgage and a social security check. The young couple is looking for long-term accumulation of wealth, possibly to save for a home, college education, or orthodontia for their children. On the other hand, the widow needs money for *today*, not 20 years from now.

This chapter is devoted to the needs of retirees, widows, and others on low "fixed" incomes, who need a supplemental income for daily living expenses that will keep up with inflation.

Traditional Sources

Traditional sources of supplemental income have included:
—*Utility stocks*, recently paying as high as 13-15 percent
—*Corporate bonds*, paying 11-12 percent
—*Government bonds*, paying 10-11 percent

—*Blue chip stocks*, "big board" stocks of major industries, paying 6-9 percent.

Recently *no-load mutual funds* have been created to simplify receiving monthly income. They invest in a variety of the income-producing vehicles mentioned above. The following is a list of representative income-producing funds:

Name of Fund	Minimum Investment	Recent Monthly Yeild
Rowe Price New Income Trust 100 East Pratt St. Baltimore, MD 21202 800-638-5660 or 301-547-2308 in Maryland	$1,000	12.8%
Fidelity Aggressive Income 82 Devonshire St. Boston, MA 02109 800-225-6190 617-726-0650 in Mass. (Also has Corporate Bond Fund, Government Securities Ltd.)	$2,500	13.0%
Dreyfus A Bonds Plus 767 Fifth Ave. New York, NY 10002 800-223-5525, or 212-935-5700 in NY	$1,000	11.3%

Utilities, bonds, stocks and mutual funds provide steady, dependable income, and your capital is relatively secure. While they do provide a better return than a savings account, the yield doesn't keep up with the cost of living.

Moreover, these income-producing vehicles tend to be poor investments in the long run, as interest rates and inflation rates climb higher. For example, in the past year, when interest rates soared to unprecedented heights, Rowe-Price's New Income Trust fell in price 7.9 percent, Fidelity's Aggressive Income fell

14.1 percent, and Dreyfus' A Bonds Plus fell 7.3 percent. These performances are representative of the entire field of income-producing investments.

Writing Call Options

Many stockbrokers have recommended writing "call options" on blue-chip stocks that customers own as a way to increase the return on their stocks. The term may seem complicated to the novice investor, but options are really quite simple.

In the stock option market, investors can buy or sell the right to purchase a stock at a future date at a specified price. Suppose the current price of a certain stock is $30, and an investor thinks the price will rise within the next six months. He buys a "call option," which allows him to buy 100 shares of that stock any time in the next six months at, say, the current $30. If the price goes up, he will exercise the option; but if it remains the same or drops, he will let the option expire. Thus, the *buyer* of a call option is speculating on the price of the stock.

So how does this increase your yield? Suppose you own 100 shares of Ford stock, selling at $30 a share and paying a 5 percent dividend. You *sell* a call option to a speculator through your broker. At present, you would receive about $350 for the sale of the option. On $3,000 worth of Ford stock, that's an additional 12 percent return—making a total return with your continued 5 percent dividend, of 17 percent.

If the price of Ford rises to, say, $100 during the next six months, the speculator who bought the option profits. He exercises the option and buys $10,000 worth of Ford stock (100 shares times $100) for $3,000—not bad for his $350 investment. On the other hand, the price may drop to $10, so that his option purchase saved you the loss of $2,000.

While writing the call option may have cost you the opportunity of earning big profits when the price rose, it also protected your capital when the price fell. No matter what, your principal investment remains the same, and you have greatly increased your yield while letting someone else gamble on the short-term price movement of the stock.

High Yield, High Growth?

Of course the best of both worlds would be to find an income-producing asset that will also increase in price, so that your net wealth increases along with your income over the long term. As long as inflation continues—and I believe that those with vested interests in inflation will see that it does—the best source today for increasing yields *and* asset value is in the natural resource stocks. Natural resources, such as oil and gas, mining, and lumber, will remain limited in production when compared to the avalanche of new paper money being printed to pay for these limited resources. Result? Higher prices over the long term. There will, of course, be cyclical downturns in the prices of the precious metals and natural resources, but the general trend will be upward during the 1980s. So my recommendation is to buy and hold, ignoring the temporary downswings, or using them as an opportunity to buy more.

Gold stocks

The highest yielding gold stocks are found in South Africa. North American stocks pay little or no dividends; as developing mines they tend to plough back as much money as possible into additional equipment and mining production.

The South African mining shares have consistently paid high dividends—most recently, yields have risen to the 15-20 percent range, even at *current* high share prices. Many sharp investors, both small and large, have seen annual yields exceed their original investments!

The secret of course is in choosing the right stock. It doesn't matter that all the others are doubling their money if the one mine you invest in has plummeted because of bad management. Big investors with plenty of money can cover these risks by diversifying into a number of mines. But for the small investor, the answer again is to find the best no-load mutual fund.

As a rule, the gold funds don't pay as high a return as do the individual gold shares. But remember that your *true yield* is based on the price you paid for the fund, not on the current price. For example, during the past year, United Services Fund has paid a 59¢ dividend. Based on the current "net asset value" ($9), that's only a 6.5 percent yield. But, if you personally had bought USF a year earlier, say July, 1979, when the price was $2.90, then your true yield would be a respectable 20 percent! (59¢ divided by $2.90).

The secret then to earning high yields on a high-growth mutual fund like United Services is to buy when the price is relatively cheap. Wait for a correction in the market before buying, for maximum yield.

Natural Resource Stocks

You could make individual purchases of oil and other natural resource stocks that have high yields, or you could buy mutual funds that specialize in natural resource stocks. Energy Fund, which we mentioned earlier, emphasizes natural resources, but pays only a small dividend (currently, 2.9 percent), because it is chiefly a growth stock. Energy Fund should be bought primarily for long-term capital gains.

Another no-load fund that currently emphasizes energy and mineral development is:

> Financial Industrial Income Fund
> Financial Programs, Inc.
> 1050 South Broadway, P. O. Box 2040
> Denver, CO 80201
> Toll-free 800-525-9831
> or 303-777-4070 in Colorado

Minimum investment is only $500. The fund is currently paying a 5.9 percent dividend, and has achieved adequate appreciation recently. Right now it is heavily invested in oil stocks.

Investing in Switzerland

Swiss franc annuities have proven to be an excellent income supplement for retired people, because the strength of the Swiss franc has provided a built-in inflation hedge.

U. S. annuities do not provide any inflationary protection at retirement. If an American annuity paid you $1,000 a month a decade ago, today it would still be paying you $1,000 a month, even though the cost of living has doubled.

Swiss annuities have a better advantage, however. Due to the continuing appreciation of the Swiss franc against the dollar, the franc has become a good inflation hedge for Americans. In 1970, the Swiss franc was worth 23 cents. Ten years later it is worth over 60 cents. While it has had some ups and downs over the years, it appreciated at a compounded annual rate of 11 percent during the past decade, and it appears that the franc will continue to move up strongly in the 1980s—as long as U. S. inflation is reckless.

So how does this affect your retirement income? When you buy an annuity, you make an agreement with an insurance company. You make a lump-sum payment to them in exchange for their promise to pay you a monthly income for the rest of your life. Since this is a fixed income, the purchasing power of your annuity (if in dollars) deteriorates with each addition to the inflation rate. But if your annuity is written in a currency that keeps up with the inflation rate, your purchasing power remains high.

For example, suppose Mr. Brown and Mr. Jones each bought annuities in 1970. Mr. Jones' policy was written in dollars, paying him $1,000 a month. Mr. Brown purchased a Swiss franc policy paying 4,310 francs per month, which was then equivalent to $1,000. Today, in 1980, Mr. Jones is still receiving $1,000 and wondering how he'll get by while Mr. Brown's 4,310 francs can be exchanged for $2,800!

In short, the traditional annuity is not a very good investment in these inflationary times. But there are a few innovative plans available, such as the Swiss franc annuities, that are worth looking into. You should expect to put up at least $30,000 to begin a Swiss annuity program.

For more detailed information, see my book, *New Profits From Insurance*, P. O. Box 611, Merrifield, VA 22116, $10. When you are serious about a Swiss annuity, contact these brokers:

International Insurance Specialists
P. O. Box 949
1211 Geneva 3, Switzerland

Assurex S. A.
P. O. Box 290
8033 Zurich, Switzerland

The Dilemma Facing Income Seekers

In summary, the income-seeker faces a difficult quandry. Either he earns high income, and suffers a deterioration of his capital, or he earns high capital gains from assets that pay few dividends. South African gold shares provide one of the few exceptions to this rule, but South Africa suffers from political uncertainty. (An embargo of South African gold, or internal riots could cut prices of S. A. golds sharply.)

Those on limited budgets who need monthly income will have to reexamine their financial goals. A steady, high monthly income that keeps up with inflation is usually a speculative and risky venture. To beat inflation, the conservative, old-time investor must learn a whole new ball game. I personally feel that socking away a few gold coins regularly, and selling them as the need arises, might be the best way to have your investments and spend them, too. But you must be the final judge of your personal financial needs.

CHAPTER 7

BEGINNER'S GUIDE
TO INTERNATIONAL
INVESTING

"The cat in gloves catches no mice."

A book on high finance would not be complete without a survey of investment opportunities around the world. There are a dozen major stock markets in Europe, Canada, the Far East, and Latin America. Prime real estate exists in such exotic places as the Caribbean, Acapulco, Hong Kong, and Monte Carlo. Gold can be bought, sold and stored in London, Montreal, Zurich, and other great cities of the world. And then there are the "Swiss gnomes," who offer truly full-service banking for independent and commercial customers. Wealthy investors have known and taken advantage of these spectacular opportunities overseas, and have invested millions outside the U. S. for diversification and safety. This chapter will introduce you to the world of international finance, and will tell you what's available for the neophyte investor.

Welcome to Swiss Banks

Swiss banks offer an incredible variety of services, far more than the limited services provided by your local "full-service"

bank. Full-service banking in Switzerland includes:
- Checking and saving accounts in *any* major world currency, e.g., U. S. dollars, British pounds, Swiss francs, German marks, Japanese yen, etc.
- Trading and storing precious metals
- Buying and selling stocks and bonds on any of the major stock exchanges around the world—Paris, London, New York, etc.
- Managed accounts in commodities, stocks, precious metals, bonds, etc.
- Safe deposit boxes
- Custodial accounts

Unlike U. S. banks, the Swiss treat your account with strictest confidentiality. They will not reveal details about your investments to anyone unless required to do so under their rigid Bank Secrecy Law.

However, the amount of money required to begin an investment program with a Swiss bank can be staggering for the uninitiated. The three major Swiss banks—Union Bank of Switzerland, Swiss Bank Corporation, and Swiss Credit Bank—all require at least $25,000 to invest in securities, precious metals, or Euromoney instruments. Managed accounts require even higher amounts—minimum 250,000 Swiss francs (or approximately $150,000 dollars).

Small Investor's Accounts

But those with surprisingly little capital can still take advantage of some Swiss accounts.

The best type of account for the small investor is the *Swiss franc savings account*. Minimums for a savings account are extremely low—most require just 100 Swiss francs ($62), and a few ask for even less. These accounts pay very little interest—currently 2½ to 3 percent annually. The interest you earn is also subject to a

35 percent withholding tax from the Swiss government, making your true yield around 2 percent.

Nevertheless, a Swiss franc savings account can prove to be an excellent inflation hedge for Americans! By putting your money into Swiss francs, you can profit from the continuing devaluation of the dollar. During the 1970s, the dollar fell dramatically against the Swiss franc and other foreign currencies because of high U. S. inflation. Meanwhile, the Swiss had little or no inflation, and the franc appreciated rapidly against the dollar from 1970-80. The following graph shows the appreciation of the Swiss franc against the dollar:

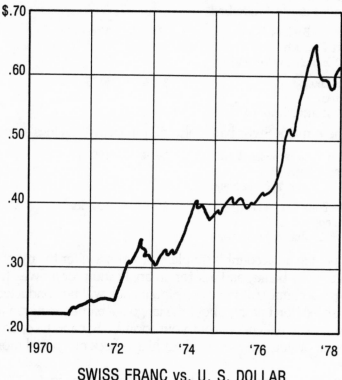

SWISS FRANC vs. U. S. DOLLAR

As the graph demonstrates, if an American had opened a Swiss franc savings account in 1970 with $1,000, today his account would be worth $2,800 *plus* interest. That return amounts to a compounded annual rate of 11 percent—substantially above the average inflation rate in the U. S. during the 1970s.

The following Swiss banks require low minimums on their Swiss franc savings accounts:

Bank	*Interest Paid*	*Minimum for Savings Account*
Migros Bank P. O. Box 2826 CH-8023 Zurich, Switzerland	2½%	None
Cantonal Bank of Zurich Briefe Postfach 8022 Zurich, Switzerland	2%	None
Bank Leu Postfach 8022 Zurich, Switzerland	2½%	$125

These major Swiss banks also permit a small savings account:

Union Bank of Switzerland Bahnhofstrasse 45 CH-8021 Zurich, Switzerland	2½%	100 SFs
Swiss Bank Corporation Paradeplatz 6 CH-8021 Zurich, Switzerland	2½%	100 SFs

Opening an account is simple. Just write a letter to any of the above Swiss banks, and ask for an application for a Swiss franc savings account. All your correspondence will be conducted in English, so don't worry about the language barrier. You can mail them a personal check from your local U. S. bank to open the account; or you can use a bank cashier's check or a postal money order.

The above banks permit you to withdraw up to 10,000 SFs

without prior notice. This policy differs from bank to bank, so that is one of the questions you will want to ask when writing for an application.

Other Swiss Services

Checking accounts. You can open a checking account at your Swiss bank with a minimum of 1,000 SFs ($620). These checking accounts are unique in that they can usually be written in any major currency of the Western world. Write a check in dollars, pounds, francs or marks. If you're traveling in England, for example, you can write a check in British pounds to pay for an item in a store. Then, in Paris, you can write a check on the same account specifying French francs. Thus, you avoid high commissions charged for foreign exchange. But unless you travel overseas, or have extensive business dealings around the world, I see little value in having a Swiss checking account.

Swiss franc endowments. Swiss life insurance companies typically pay higher returns on Swiss franc investments than do Swiss banks. They sell "endowment policies," which are like bank certificates of deposit, except that they are sold by an insurance company. Under this arrangement, you invest a specified amount, say, 10,000 Swiss francs. The endowment earns interest and dividends at a rate of 4-5 percent a year, and at maturity, you are paid a lump sum from the insurance company. Endowments can run from 1 to 15 years—it's up to you to decide the time to maturity. Minimum investment is 10,000 SFs, or about $6,200. For further information, contact the Swiss insurance brokers referred to in Chapter 6, or see my book, *New Profits From Insurance*.

Coins and bullion. Swiss banks require a much higher minimum for buying bullion or coins—typically $10,000 to $25,000. Of course, you can buy a single coin if you appear in person at the gold window of the bank. But it's a different story by mail. For the small investor, I suggest that you continue buying coins or bullion at home through a coin dealer, bank or broker such as Merrill Lynch. Merrill Lynch's Gold Sharebuilders Plan, recommended in Chapter 4, stores the gold for you in London. Citibank's and Deak's gold purchase plans store gold for you in Zurich, Switzerland, or in London or the U. S. So you can still have small amounts of gold stored for you in Europe even though you make your purchase in the states.

The same high minimums apply in the case of buying stocks offered on foreign stock markets. Plan on using a Swiss banker as your broker only if you have $25,000 or more to invest. Otherwise, the small investor is limited to using U. S.-based brokers or mutual funds to invest in overseas stocks.

Most Swiss banks also have branches located in the Bahamas and the Cayman Islands in the Caribbean. There you can open a Swiss franc savings account with the advantages of being physically close to the U. S., and also avoiding the 35 percent withholding tax on interest earnings, as well as avoiding any restrictions the Swiss may impose on foreign accounts from time to time. (In the mid-1970s, when the franc was in heavy demand, the Swiss government imposed a "negative" interest penalty on large Swiss accounts. However, these penalties never applied to Swiss branches in the Caribbean). The minimum investment is higher in the islands, however—typically $5,000 or more. For details, write:

Bank Leu International   Swiss Credit Bank
P. O. Box N3926   P. O. Box N4928
Nassau, the Bahamas   Nassau, the Bahamas

Will the Swiss Franc Remain a Good Inflation Hedge?

Will the Swiss franc continue to appreciate at an 11 percent average annual rate during the 1980s? I believe it will continue to be a good inflation hedge for Americans. The Swiss dislike inflation intensely—they can tolerate 5 percent a year at most. Swiss monetary authorities have made every effort to hold down growth in the money supply and to avoid federal deficits. Contrast this to the U. S. government, which has shown no real effort to restrict federal spending or monetary growth. I expect double-digit inflation to continue in the U. S., and the growing disparity between U. S. and Swiss inflation will mean a weaker dollar and a stronger franc.

Despite seemingly low interest rates, a Swiss franc savings account will prove to be a worthwhile investment for small savers. The key factor to watch is the inflation rate in both countries. For statistics on the inflation rate in most foreign countries, including Switzerland, the Federal Reserve Bank of St. Louis offers a free publication. Write to:

> International Economic Conditions
> Federal Reserve Bank of St. Louis
> P. O. Box 442
> St. Louis, MO 63166

Currently, the Swiss franc is selling for about 62¢. I believe that in the not-too-distant future, the Swiss franc will be exchanged on par, $1 equal to SF1.

Investing In Other World Currencies

The Swiss franc remains the world's hardest currency because of its consistently low inflation rate. Over the long term, I would expect the franc to outperform all other world currencies.

There are other currencies, however, that will offer good short-term speculations, either because of high interest rates or because they are appreciating against the dollar.

German mark

While the Swiss franc moved up 11 percent annually against

the dollar in the 1970s, the German mark appreciated at a respectable rate of 8 percent. And interest rates tend to be slightly higher on German mark savings accounts—banks typically pay 7-8 percent per annum. The German mark will continue to appreciate against the dollar in the 1980s if Germany maintains an inflation rate below that of the U. S. The Swiss banks mentioned earlier offer savings accounts in any currency, including German marks. Check with them for account applications.

British pound

The British pound sterling has been remarkably strong against the dollar over the past 5 years. It fell to as low as $1.70 in the mid-1970s, but has since regained its value and moved up to around $2.40. The factors that have contributed to this resurgence in strength have been the discovery of North Sea oil, election of a Conservative government, and a stricter monetary policy that has pushed interest rates up. Currently, savings accounts in Britain are paying 15 percent interest per annum! I doubt that this high rate will continue indefinitely, however, so I would consider this a short-term speculation. The British have not yet proven that they will hold down government spending over the long run, so you can't invest in the pound and forget it. It has to be monitored continually.

Again, you can open up a British pound savings account at your Swiss bank, or if you prefer to have one in London, write:

National Westminster Bank Ltd.
41 Lothbury
London EC2P 2BP, England

Foreign Currency Travelers Checks

Another simple way to hold money in a foreign currency is to purchase the banknotes themselves, or travelers checks, at a local bank or foreign exchange office. Of course you won't earn any interest this way, but the main reason for investing in hard currencies is to take advantage of their appreciation against the dollar. Travelers checks are insured against loss or theft, and sometimes can be bought without the 1 percent commission (e.g., Deak-Perera Co.). You can buy American Express travelers checks in most major currencies, from the Swiss franc to the British pound, with as little as two hundred dollars.

If you can't find a local dealer, you can buy travelers checks directly by mail from:

Deak-Perera Co.
29 Broadway
New York, NY 10006

How to Invest in the Eurocurrency Market

Multinational investors often speculate in a wider variety of currencies available on the Euromarket. Currencies available for trading include: German marks, Dutch guilders, Swiss francs, Japanese yen, pound sterling, or U. S. dollars. Typically the Eurocurrency markets pay higher interest rates (for example, Swiss francs are currently paying 5½ percent on 3-month certificates) because of the risk from the European borrowers. It's a totally free market in currencies, governed only by supply and demand. Certificates are offered for 3-month, 6-month, and 9-month periods.

Most Swiss banks won't let you speculate in the Euromarket for less than $25,000, but the following trust company in Canada has a minimum requirement of $5,000:

Guardian Trust Company
87 Yonge St.
Toronto, Ontario M5C 1S8
Telephone 416-863-1100

What About the Mexican Peso?

Many American investors have heard about the high interest paid on Mexican-peso certificates of deposit and wonder: Are they worth the risk?

While dollar interest rates have fallen from their early 1980 highs, the Mexican peso yields have climbed to an incredibly 25 percent currently being paid on 2-year certificates. Here is the breakdown on Mexican peso yields as of November 1980:

MEXICAN PESO YIELDS

Time Period	Net Interest Rate
7-day Deposit	13.5%
30-day Deposit	16.9%
3-month Deposit	18.5%
6-month Deposit	19.75%
1-Year Deposit	22.7%
2-Year Deposit	25.6%

Minimum investment is as small as $1,000 (or 25,000 pesos) at some Mexican banks.

The major concern when investing in the peso is its stability. Mexico has recently become a large oil producer, which has helped in its balance of payments. But the inflation rate in Mexico has persistently exceeded the U. S. rate, and pressure is mounting for further devaluations. In 1976 the Mexican government devalued the peso by 40 percent, and many American investors lost their shirts. Mexico is now engaging in a series of mini-devaluations, which will lower your return in real terms. How long this will continue is anyone's guess. Consider Mexican peso CDs a risky speculation.

You can avoid the risks of devaluation by investing your funds in a U. S. dollar account in Mexico, but the interest rates are much lower, about 11 percent, and the minimum is currently around $8,000.

You can open a dollar or peso account at any major Mexican bank, such as Comermex, Banamex, or Somex. A medium-sized bank specializing in American clients is:

Banca Metropolitana
Attn: Eugene Latham, *Mexletter*
Apartado 1339
Mexico 1, D. F., Mexico
905-512-4890

When you open an account, you also receive Eugene Latham's informative monthly letter, *Mexletter*. (Normally $20 a year).

How to Invest in Foreign Stocks

While the U. S. stock market may be floundering from time to time, foreign stock markets may be flourishing. In the recent past, stocks have skyrocketed in London, Mexico City, Paris, and other financial centers around the world. How can you profit? You could buy the stocks directly, or you could buy into the mutual funds that are promoted by major banks in Germany, Mexico, etc. But most of these are "load" or commissioned funds, are not registered in the U. S., and require frequent long-distance communication. I don't recommend them for the small investor.

Internationally-oriented mutual funds do exist in the U. S. and might be a more convenient and less costly way to profit from Foreign stocks. The mutual fund with the best record in this field is:

Templeton Growth Fund
41 Beach Dr. SE
St. Petersburg, FL 33701
800-237-0738
or 813-823-8712 in Florida

According to its literature, a $10,000 investment in the

Templeton Fund in 1954 reached $268,000 in 1980! The fund is a load fund, requiring an 8½ percent commission, and of course future performance depends entirely upon the astuteness of its money managers. *Forbes* rated it "A" in up markets and "A+" in down markets. Minimum investment is just $500.

Scudder International Fund is a no-load fund investing in foreign stocks. Its record has not been as consistent as Templeton's, but it has made good returns over all. Fortunately, it has a telephone switch feature with a toll-free 800 number, so you can transfer your money immediately into a money market fund if you foresee a change in the market. Minimum investment is $1,000. Write:

> Scudder International Fund
> 345 Park Ave.
> New York, NY 10022
> Toll-free 800-225-2470
> or 212-350-8200 in NY

There are other alternatives as well. G. T. Pacific Fund, a no-load mutual fund in San Francisco, specializes in Far East securities. Its performance has been lackluster so far. The Japan Fund, a closed-end stock fund traded on the New York Exchange, has performed admirably over the past decade. It must be purchased through a broker.

South African mining shares can be purchased easily and with little investment through United Services Fund, (no-load) International Investors, (load) or ASA (a closed-end stock fund).

Hundreds of individual foreign stocks from Europe, Asia, Africa, Canada and Latin America are available on American stock exchanges as American Depository Receipts (ADRs). But I wouldn't recommend them to the small investor, who needs to diversify and spread the risk of ownership.

Summary

You too can profit from overseas investing, whether you have $100 or $10,000. You can open a small savings account in Swiss francs, German marks, British pounds, or other major currencies by using a Swiss bank. Foreign stocks, which often outperform American stocks, are readily available through mutual funds. You can have hard assets like gold and silver stored for you in reputable foreign banks.

Diversification is the watchword in these uncertain times. It pays to have a small portion of your nest egg in foreign investments, to protect your assets from an economic crisis that could strike at any time in this country, or elsewhere around the world.

CHAPTER 8

REAL ESTATE WITH LITTLE DOWN

"Patience in market is worth pounds in a year."

Owning a home has always been the American dream. But today the most common worry of young people and those just starting out is that the American dream will always be beyond their reach. Home prices and mortgage rates are rising so fast that by the time they have enough money scraped together for the downpayment, the price has gone up again to where they still can't afford it. It seems like a never-ending climb up a never-ending ladder.

But there are ways of attaining that dream, however elusive it may seem. This chapter will help you down the road to home ownership, and will also give you some tips on investing in real estate as a source of income and capital appreciation.

There are basically three ways to lower your costs when searching for that dream home. One, of course, is to find a house with a lower price. The second is to make a large downpayment, so your monthly payments are lower. The third, and the one we will concentrate on the most, is to utilize creative new financing techniques that can lower your monthly payments without requiring a huge downpayment.

Why Buy?

Buying a home can be one of the most important investment decisions you make. And in an inflationary environment, the sooner you buy, the better off you'll be. The tax advantages are superior. All interest payments and property taxes are deductible if you itemize. Eventually you can trade up into a larger home, and you can defer all your capital gains taxes if you buy within 18 months of the time you sell your previous home. When you reach 55 years of age or older, you can sell your home and take a once-in-a-lifetime tax-free profit of up to $100,000. If your home has appreciated by more than $100,000, the difference is taxed as long term capital gains, which are 60 percent tax free.

From an investment point of view, your home offers a fairly stable investment. Salomon Brothers ranked it 11th among all investments during the decade of the 70s, with an annual appreciation of 10.2 percent nationwide—substantially above the consumer price index increase of 7.7 percent. This means that most homes more than doubled in price in ten years. When you consider the fact that many people actually invest just 10 percent as the initial downpayment, the return on the original investment is phenomenal.

Now that we have established that buying a home is a solid investment idea, how do you go about it?

First you must recognize that despite the rise in housing prices, homes still differ considerably in value. If the average home costs close to $70,000 nationally, at least half the homes in the country must be selling for less. You may not be able to buy your dream home right away, but at least you can get started. The new buyer with little money should consider the following lower-priced homes:

- Condominiums
- Townhouses
- Cooperative apartments (in Northeast U. S.)

● Older, smaller homes in need of repair

No matter where you live, there are bargains, selling at far below the national or local average. And you aren't necessarily limited to run-down homes in neighborhoods fifty miles from town. Many builders, caught in the credit crunch, are currently selling off their new homes at much lower prices, just to get rid of them. Make him an offer—he might just accept it!

Unusual Property Values

But the individual with little money and a low budget should begin by searching for the following situations:

—*Auctions on condominiums.* Auctions occur from time to time in overbuilt areas, where supply has outgrown demand. Florida and big cities in the East have experienced recent examples. Builders and promoters are on a tight sales schedule and can't afford to hold onto properties for more than several months. Time is on your side, therefore, and if your condo is in a good area the demand will eventually catch up to the supply. I attended such an auction near Washington, D. C., and saw nice 2- and 3-bedroom condos selling for $20,000 to $30,000 below the retail asking price (the price which most of the present occupants paid!). The builder required only a 10 percent downpayment, amounting to as little as $5,000.

Now, just a few years later, these condos are selling for several thousand dollars above the original *retail* price, a profit of $30,000 to $40,000 for those shrewd investors who bought at auction. A condo is not a bad way to get started in home-buying, as long as you are willing to hold it for a few years.

—*Small, older homes in need of repair.* Little two-bedroom homes on small lots can be purchased at prices substantially lower than the national average. If the home is in need of repair, it won't sell as fast, and the owner may be willing to accept a low offer. If the seller has a great deal of equity, or owns it outright, he may even be willing to take back the mortgage himself, with little or no money down, especially if he is a retiree in need of supplemental income. Don't be afraid to negotiate!

By fixing up the home cosmetically, you can add thousands to its selling value. Thus, without spending a lot of money, you can soon "trade up" to a larger home.

—*Government-Assisted Homes.* Most government-subsidized housing is located in the inner city, often in unsafe areas, and frankly looks like low-income housing. But there are ways of buying a middle-class home in a nice neighborhood while still taking advantage of government-assisted programs.

Recently many county governments have made money for low-interest mortages available to middle-income families. But because the amount of money is very limited, it often takes a tenacious spirit to discover where the money is, how much is available, and how you can qualify. Usually the county does not loan the money itself, but puts you in touch with lenders who have previously agreed to set aside a certain amount of money to loan to qualifying borrowers at low interest rates. Qualifications vary, but generally your income should be between $15,000-$25,000, you should have a good credit rating with little debt, and it helps if you're married. It helps even more if you have children.

Unlike low-income housing, which is built and financed by the state, these programs cover financing only—you find the home through regular channels in ordinary neighborhoods. You thus avoid the stigma and possible resale problems of living in a low-income or subsidized neighborhood.

Creative Financing

As home prices and interest rates have skyrocketed, new methods of financing mortgages have become popular, resulting in lower monthly payments or a lower downpayment, or both. Here are just a few of the latest ideas:

● *Owner financing at below market rates.* In some cases the owners may be willing to finance all or part of your loan themselves. They may be in a hurry to sell and you are their only prospect. Or perhaps they don't need the money from the sale in full right away but would rather have a regular income. Whatever the reason, don't be afraid to ask the seller what kind of financial arrangements he can make for you. Not many sellers are willing or able to finance the whole house, but many will take back a second mortgage for the difference between what the bank will lend you and the selling price.

Another technique used recently is an arrangement whereby the owner sells the home only, and then *leases* the land to the buyer. This way the price is substantially lower. But be very careful in using this technique that you have all your rights and obligations spelled out in a legal contract. In particular, you would want to have a long-term lease on which the rent cannot escalate, or an option to buy the land at a future date at a reasonable price.

● *Profit-sharing or joint ownership.* This is a novel idea whereby the mortgage company agrees to charge you a below-market interest rate in exchange for a share in the future appreciation of the home. Advance Mortgage Corporation in Detroit is offering such mortgages in a select group of cities throughout the U. S. For example, the mortgage company might reduce the interest rates by a third, say from 14 percent to 10 percent, in exchange for a third share of the profits when you sell your home a few years later. If the price increases by $30,000, they would receive $10,000.

Another variation of this idea is joint ownership, whereby a real estate company would become your *partner* in buying the home. The firm would help pay the closing costs, downpayment, and monthly mortgage payments. In return, it would get

50 percent of the profits when the home is sold. Home Partners of America, Inc., is one firm offering this service.

● *Variable payments.* Most people find that their incomes rise each year, through raises, promotions, and cost-of-living increases. Consequently, many mortgage companies and banks are now experimenting with ways to allow the owner to make smaller payments in the first few years when income is lower, and higher payments later on, when the ability to pay has increased. Typically this involves either variable interest rates, or graduated payments at a pre-determined rate. With the former, your mortgage starts out with a below-market interest rate. It is reassessed periodically, perhaps every three years, and is linked to the current rate charged for new mortgages. Since interest rates are likely to continue their upward climb, this technique could end up costing you a lot of money. With the graduated-payment plan, you know in advance exactly how much your payments will be for the ensuing years. I would recommend this plan over the variable-interest plan.

Reducing Closing Costs

Settlement costs can astound you, especially the first time around. Don't be shocked if it amounts to as much as 5 percent of the amount you are borrowing! Some of the items are negotiable, however, so ask for a breakdown of the fees in advance so you can do some shopping. The lawyer's fee, for example, can vary by as much as $500. Also, if your seller is in a hurry to close the deal and doesn't have any other prospects, he may be willing to pay for part or all of the closing costs himself, or to figure them into the price of the house so you don't have to come up with as much cash.

The seller gets hit even harder at settlement time. In addition to all the state-required fees, lawyer's fees, prepayment penalties, and so forth, the seller must also pay the broker's fee of 6 percent of the price of the house. Sometimes you can negotiate with a real estate agent to lower the fee to 5 percent, but they don't like to do it.

Many people avoid the broker's fee altogether by selling their homes themselves. The savings may be elusive, however. Often a buyer, knowing you are saving that 6 percent, will expect you to lower your price substantially, cutting into your expected profits. And there are many valid services offered by real estate agents, such as multiple listing, professionally showing your home, knowledge of necessary forms, finding financing for the buyer, and just plain experience.

If, however, your home is in excellent condition, in a prime neighborhood, with good exposure, then by all means plant a "For Sale by Owner" sign. There are several good books on the market which could be helpful if you decide to sell your own home. One I recommend is *How to Sell Your Home Without a Real Estate Broker*, by Carl J. Kosner (McGraw-Hill Books, 1221 Ave. of the Americas, New York, NY 10020, $10.95). You can always list your house with an agent later if it doesn't work out.

Discount Brokers

One way to have the best of both worlds; that is, to have the services of a broker without paying thousands of dollars, is to use one of the new discount brokers available in many major cities. These alternative brokers are being franchised throughout the nation, and may eventually force conventional agents to lower their standard commission rates. These brokers offer the same services as a conventional agent including multiple listing, paper work, newspaper ads, etc. Two such organizations are Home Sellers Center Inc., out of Atlanta, and Save-Com out of Arizona. They are fixed-fee brokers, charging between $350 and $700 per listing, depending on the area where you live. They do everything except show the house. Their success rate is about 75 percent nationwide, though I suspect that the rate improves during good times when demand is higher. Check the phone book under real estate brokers in your area.

Low-Risk Real Estate Investing

There has been a great deal of publicity lately about the phenomenal profits to be made in residential and commercial real estate—even by the little investor. Crash courses in creative real estate that tell you how to pyramid your hard-earned money into a small fortune are being advertised in major cities throughout the country. It looks like a sure deal, if you can ever get your foot in the door.

There is a lot of money to be made in real estate, but it isn't as easy as these writers and speakers would have you believe. While success stories abound, the failures are usually overlooked. There are numerous cases of investors who have purchased apartments that couldn't remain fully rented, or who bought in areas that proved to be in decline economically, or who bought at the top of the market and were hit by the recession. In addition, real estate investments require that you borrow a lot of money, which can keep you awake nights. If you think that owning a piece of real estate is the only way to financial success, think again (and reread my chapters on gold, stocks, and foreign investments)!

Selected wisely, however, and financed creatively, real estate can be a good source of additional income. But I recommend that the low-budget investor begin his portfolio by purchasing some of the sound investments mentioned in earlier chapters, such as gold, mutual funds, and hard currencies, first. Then, with a good foundation of hard assets, you are ready to enter the area of income-producing property.

Investing in Residential Property

Residential property is probably the best place for you to get started because it is in plentiful supply with high demand. This means you should be able to turn it over fairly quickly. There are some simple, tried-and-true steps that can help you select the right property and prepare it for renting or resale.

Step #1. Buy a small residential property that is undervalued. "Small residential property" refers to a single-family home, condominium, townhouse, duplex or fourplex. I would stay completely away from commercial property, raw land, or farm land, which is harder to sell and more difficult to finance. Commercial property, such as an office building, may seem appealing because it can provide "cash flow," where your rent revenue is greater than your mortgage and operating costs. But during a recession, when offices are hard to rent, you can be stuck with a heavy mortgage and not enough money to meet the payments. Residential property is far more stable and suitable for the small investor.

"Undervalued property" refers to a house or property that is located in a good area but is run-down or in need of upgrading. You can buy it at a distressed price because most prospective buyers are turned off by the appearance of the house. It may need paint, a new driveway, an improved lawn, more modern kitchen appliances, new carpet, or a host of other cosmetic improvements. It is absolutely imperative, however, that this kind of house be located in a decent neighborhood. You're searching for the small substandard home in an otherwise standard neighborhood. Don't buy the run-down home or fourplex found in a neighborhood full of run-down homes.

Step #2. Make cosmetic improvements that don't cost a great deal. You should be looking for property that has a solid foundation, something that would be quite desirable *if* it were fixed up. Ideally your repairs should increase the value of the property by several times more than the cost of the improvements.

Real estate experts agree that the following types of cosmetic changes can add a great deal to the resale value of a piece of real estate:

- Paint and wallpaper
- Simple landscaping
- Cleanup (grounds, basement, interior)
- Replacement of outdated fixtures
- Replacement of carpet
- New kitchen and bathroom fixtures, floors, etc.
- New drapes or clean existing ones
- New or refurbished front door

None of the above items will be too expensive when compared to the value they add to your property.

There are certain other kinds of improvements you should avoid that generally will not increase the value significantly. These include adding a swimming pool, garage, storm-windows, luxury appliances such as trash compactors, a new roof, finished basement, or a barbeque.

Real estate experts consider the kitchen and bathroom to be the most important rooms when showing a house or apartment. Improvements in these areas will prove to be the most profitable when seeking a quick resale.

Step #3. Sell the residential property, and use the profits to make larger purchases. Even if real estate prices are softer at the time you sell, your cosmetic improvements will bring you substantial profits. Use these profits to purchase larger "undervalued" homes, using higher leverage (greater debt) for maximum profits.

The residential-property, fix-up approach is the safest, soundest way to build a small fortune in real estate. It is the basic technique that is promoted in greater detail for hundreds of dollars at weekend seminars around the country. If you want more information, I suggest you read Al Lowry's book, *How You Can Become Financially Independent by Investing in Real Estate* (Simon &

Schuster, 630 Fifth Ave., New York, NY 10020, $10), or for the more adventuresome speculator, *Nothing Down,* by Robert G. Allen (Simon & Schuster, $10).

A word of caution is in order, however, about the "creative" approach to real estate. It can get you into trouble. Buying real estate with "no money down" or sometimes buying real estate with "more than 100 percent financing" (where you end up with money in your pocket), can spell trouble down the road. Sometimes the speculative artist can play the real estate game as long as he can pay the interest, while he counts on inflation to bring him through in the end. But you can't always count on inflation, except to raise your costs!

That's why I recommend that your own home be your primary real estate investment. Income-producing is not for everyone, and it may well not be for you.

Owning a Resort Condominium At Holiday Inn Prices

How would you like to own a resort condominium in some such exotic place as Acapulco, Hawaii, or Lake Tahoe? Seem like an impossible dream? You might not be able to own it outright, but now, finally, there is a way for the average investor to profit along with the wealthy from the tremendous rise in resort condo prices.

How? By investing in time-sharing condos! Under a time-sharing plan, you purchase a week or two weeks of vacation time at a resort condominium for the next 25 years. Generally you pay around 4-10 times the normal weekly rental price. Prices are as low as $1,000, and as high as $30,000, depending on the location of the resort, the condition of the condo, additional services, and the time of year. The average price is about $4,000.

What are the risks? First, time-sharing prices may be inflated when compared to the cost of owning the entire condo. Also, most time-sharing plans are not purchased so much for an investment as for vacation enjoyment. If you're interested in it primarily for speculation, you should avoid those plans that give you a specified "interest" in the condo, but not direct ownership. You want to buy into a time-sharing plan that gives you direct ownership, thus allowing you to sell your share to someone else for a profit. Under ownership arrangements, you can sell or rent your time as you please.

Incidentally, if you decide to use your condo rather than rent it, exchange organizations have been set up to allow you to exchange your resort condo for one in another area, so you don't have to vacation in the same place for the next 25 years! Exchanging time-shares is becoming increasingly popular.

Overall, time-sharing seems to have caught on. Sales have doubled every year since its creation in 1976. For more information, you should write: "Buyers Guide to Resort Time-Sharing," C. H. B. Company, P. O. Box 184, Los Altos, CA 94022, $7. Or, a small brochure is available for 50 cents (plus a self-addressed stamped business-size envelope) from Resort Time-Sharing Council, 100 16th St., N. W., Washington, D. C. 20036 (or call 202-659-4582).

Have a great vacation—and a profitable one too!

Second Deed Trusts

An often-overlooked way to profit from real estate is by becoming a lender rather than a buyer. Second mortgates or second deed trusts can be a good investment from time to time as long as you keep your eyes wide open. A second mortgage is arranged when a buyer can't close the gap between the downpayment and the amount allowed by the lender for the first mortgage. Usually the real estate agent, in order to close the sale, will find a third party, an investor, who is willing to make up the difference in the form of a second mortgage. Because of the higher risk, yields on second trusts tend to be higher over those on first mortgages, and tend to mature sooner, generally in 2-5 years. During early 1980, when rates on first mortgages went as high as 17 percent, holders of second mortgages were getting 20-24 percent annual return on their money!

Second mortgages vary considerably. They can be written (purchased) for as little as $1,000, although most are for $5,000 or so. Second mortgages are "discounted" to the buyer. In other words, a second trust that has a $5,000 value at maturity may be sold for $4,000 to the investor. By holding the trust deed to maturity, the investor gets the full $5,000, plus interest. Second mortgages seldom mature in more than 5 years, or less than 2 years. So, if you invest in a second, you should be willing to hold it until maturity for maximum profit. The market for second trusts is relatively liquid, meaning that you can usually find a buyer if you need to sell, but when interest rates are rising sharply, your second trust will be heavily discounted if you try to sell early.

How to get started? Contact several reliable real estate agents and let them know you have some money to invest in second mortgages. Agents will contact you when they have a situation where they can use more cash to close the deal.

Some warnings: Don't take the word of the agent. Check over the financial situation of the real estate buyer yourself. Make sure he puts up a healthy downpayment, and that his financial condition is good. Your risk lies in the possibility of default on the part of the owner—if the house or property must be sold, the holder of the first mortgage gets paid before you do.

Second mortgages can be a great way to lock into a temporarily high interest rate. A friend of mine recently bought a 3-year, $5,000 second trust for a discounted $3,500. The trust pays 12 percent interest, plus a substantial capital gain of $1,500 at maturity. His overall return will be slightly over 20 percent.

Shortly after he got the second trust, interest rates fell back sharply, so his investment was well-timed.

Second deed trusts are a high-risk investment because of the possibility of default. The very fact that the buyer needs a second mortgage tends to indicate that his financial situation is fairly tight. I wouldn't jump in unless the speculative opportunity is unusually good, and even then it would not represent a majority of my investment portfolio.

Real Estate Investment Trusts (REITs)

Another way of investing in real estate without the headaches associated with physical ownership is through the purchase of trust funds called Real Estate Investment Trusts (REITs). Like mutual funds, these trusts pool the resources of numerous investors and then purchase large apartment complexes, office buildings, shopping malls, and other commercial property. REITs are available on the stock market in the over-the-counter market and are traded daily. Many, such as Property Trust of America and Connecticut General, sell for as little as $10-$25 a share, making real estate affordable for even the smallest investor.

REITs have some excellent tax advantages, too. Equity-type REITs, which actually own property, can pass on much of their dividends as either a long-term capital gain, which is 60-percent tax free, or as a return of capital, which is entirely tax free!

This does not apply to mortgage-type REITs, which I feel should be avoided. Mortgage REITs lend money to real estate developers, but do not generally own the actual property. To take advantage of higher real estate prices, I would buy only equity-type REITs.

What about past performance? Ah, there's the rub! Equity REITs have had their ups and downs. They performed extremely well, tripling in value, in the early 1970s, but then crashed in

1974 when the recession and high interest rates hit. Since then, they have recouped some of their losses, but they have not regained their 1973 highs. It is important to know that equity-type REITs invest primarily in commercial property, which is the most volatile of all real estate ventures. So if you do buy REITs, plan on being a trader, and not a long-term holder.

You can buy REITs through a discount broker if you know something about them and can choose specific stocks. Otherwise contact a full-service broker who specializes in REITs. You can also get some general information and a list of REITs by writing to the National Association of Real Estate Investment Trusts, 1101 17th St., NW, Washington, D. C. 20036 ($4 for their current issue of REIT Industry Monthly Review).

Real Estate: The Final Word

As long as inflation continues in this country, real estate belongs in your investment portfolio. Your personal residence may be your only investment in this field, or you may want to branch out into some of the more speculative areas of real estate investments mentioned in this chapter.

Becaue of the volatility of our economy today, I believe that many investors who have put too much of their money into real estate, thinking it's a "sure deal," will be caught short of cash and will have to bail out someday. But by taking the more moderate approach I have described, the small investor can limit his risks and still make a good deal of money.

CHAPTER 9

$100 GETS YOU STARTED IN ART AND COLLECTIBLES

"Wealth is not his that has it,
but his that enjoys it."

The homes of the wealthy are often filled with lovely furnishings or exotic hobbies that not only bring daily pleasure to the owners but prove to be profitable investments as well. The average person on a low budget, however, has generally had to settle for cheap copies of period pieces, and such less expensive hobbies as collecting bottle caps or beer cans, because the exorbitant prices of antiques, stamps, art, and other collectibles were simply too high.

Throughout the 1970s, collectibles were in a feverish bull market. Salomon Brothers' survey of inflation hedges lists stamps, Chinese ceramics, rare books, diamonds, and old masters as just a few of the many collectible fields that exploded during the past decade of inflation. News headlines reported record prices at the major auction houses in New York and London. A Rembrandt painting sold for $5 million. A U. S. gold doubloon was auctioned off at the unexpected price of $436,000. The famous upside-down-airplane stamp was purchased for a quarter of a million. Only the super-rich can afford these prices.

But there are many other stories that go unreported in the newspapers, stories of lower-priced items that quietly continue to increase in value without any fanfare. By gaining a working knowledge of the subject, even those on the tightest budgets can enter the collectibles market, purchasing items for as little as $100 that will eventually be worth thousands.

What to Buy

Knowledge is your most important asset when investing in art and other collectibles. The more you know about what makes an item valuable, the better chance you will have of finding top quality at a rock-bottom price. You won't find Alladin's lamp in a junk store unless you already know a great deal about Arabian brassworks—and a little bit about genies as well.

Of course you can't expect to become an expert on all the possible art forms and collector's items available. Even the professionals rely on one another to specialize. This is the one investment area where diversification is not the key to risk-free speculation.

You need to select one specific area that is appealing to you and then learn everything there is to know about it. If you like Oriental rugs, for example, you should eventually be able to determine where it was made, just by looking at the design; how it was made, by examining the type of knot; when it was made, by determining the source of the dyes; and how well it was made, by counting the knots-per-square-inch. Additionally, you will keep up-to-date on current auction prices. All this information is available at the public library.

You may choose to specialize in something you already know about, or something you already have in your possession, or something you enjoy. If you're a deer hunter, for instance, you might want to collect antique firearms. Your collectibles will give you both capital appreciation and personal enjoyment.

Where to Buy: Auctions Versus Dealers

As you become an expert in your field, you may find someone locally who is both reasonable and reliable to deal with.
However, my general recommendation is to avoid local dealers
and deal only through the large, well-known auction houses at
first. Numismatic coins, old jewelry, antique firearms, rare
books, and old paintings can easily be overvalued or even
counterfeited by unscrupulous dealers. This is a field replete
with con artists, so you must be constantly on guard. If it sounds
too good to be true, it probably is!

Two reputable auction houses are:

Sotheby Parke Bernet
980 Park Ave.   34 New Bond St., W.1
New York, NY 10021   London, England
212-472-3400

Christie's
502 Park Ave.   8 King St.
New York, NY 10022   London, England
212-546-1000   SW1Y 6QT

You don't have to go to New York or London to deal
through them, however. All major auction houses accept bids
by mail. You simply send them the maximum price you are
willing to pay for an item, and they bid for you against other
prospective buyers. They are quite reputable and will make sure
you get the best price possible, even if it's lower than the
amount they know you are willing to spend.

Sotheby's and Christie's both publish catalogs throughout the
year that give you a detailed description of what will be
available at upcoming auctions. Different catalogs are published
for each collectible category, such as books, paintings, wines,
rugs, autographs, coins, ceramics, etc. You can send for a free list
of these catalogs, which will include a detailed breakdown of the

categories and the prices charged for each catalog. Sotheby's also publishes a newsletter which announces upcoming auctions and mentions special items that will be featured. The newsletter is $3 a year.

In addition to describing the items for sale, the catalog will usually list an estimated price, which is the approximate price the seller hopes to get. Your maximum bid should be about 10 percent over the estimated price. The auctioneer then bids for you as though you were actually there, so your competitors never realize that you have already established a maximum. The auction house is paid a commission by the seller, usually 10 percent of the actual price. Sometimes the buyer is required to pay a commission as well.

Bidding by mail has the added advantage of avoiding "auction fever" when an inexperienced bidder can get caught up in the excitement and spend far more than he had intended. If you do attend auctions in person be sure to set yourself a limit before the bidding begins and stick to it, no matter how sure you are that the competing buyer is going to drop out after the very next bid.

How to Choose A Collectible

Even after you have narrowed the collectible field to a single area of expertise, you are still faced with having to choose from among hundreds of possible purchases. The following guidelines will help you to choose a winner.

First, stay with quality. Good pieces hold their value better than poor-quality items, and also sell better at auction. Don't be penny-wise and dollar-foolish when it comes to quality.

Second, look for beauty. Beautiful objects always sell well, and can give you much aesthetic pleasure over the years if you decide to keep them.

Third, stay away from modern art. Whether you're investing in stamps, legal tender coins, medallions, paintings, or prints, stick with the rare or old item—don't buy newly-issued collectibles at high retail prices. You want an object with a proven track record, not something that is likely to sell at below the original price in a few years. Especially beware of the artificial "limited editions" of silver ingots, Christmas plates, "rare" books, coins, etc. While a few issues have proven successful, most have not.

Fourth, look for a ready market. Don't buy into an exotic field that only a handful of investors are interested in. Stay with the proven collectibles which have plenty of potential buyers around the country and around the world. Faddish markets should also be avoided—they're too unpredictable for long-term profits. (A 1952 Mickey Mantle baseball card sold for $2,000 at a 1979 auction, only to sell for $300 in 1980).

Fifth, plan on holding for several years. When you pay 10-15 percent commissions on collectibles, you have to plan on holding them for several years in order to make optimal long-term capital gains. This is not an in-and-out market.

Best Buys for the Small Investor

Let's take a closer look at a few collectible markets that offer the best opportunities for the novice investor who wants fast appreciation on smaller-priced items.

Rare coins

Rare or numismatic gold and silver coins can still be purchased individually for under $1,000—and even a few for under $300—but most gold coins that are both rare and in uncirculated condition are much more expensive.

There are three main categories describing the condition of rare coins: proof, brilliant uncirculated, and circulated. "Proof" coins are the most rare and consequently the most expensive. They are coins that were set aside for collectors immediately after being struck, and have absolutely no blemishes or marks on them. "Brilliant uncirculated" (BU) coins never circulated in public either, but they were not set aside and may be scratched with "bag marks" from mint bags. "Circulated" coins are also graded, depending on wear and tear.

I recommend the purchase of gold coins in brillant uncirculated condition (BU)—specifically the $20 Liberty and St. Gauden double-eagles, the $10 Liberty or Indian eagles, and the $5 half-eagles. You should always buy rare coins in BU condition—it pays to stay with quality. But the small investor should generally stay away from proof coins as they are too rare and consequently too expensive.

The best coins for the beginner are the rare silver coins. Prices on silver start considerably lower than on gold, although admittedly even silver coins have skyrocketed over the past few years. Historically, rare silver coins have outperformed the bullion or "junk" silver, while avoiding the gut-wrenching drops that occur in the bullion price of silver from time to time.

There are numberous ways to invest. I suggest you diversify as much as possible while still remaining within an area of expertise. Some general categories might include:

—individual Morgan silver dollars, Franklin halves, Washington quarters, Mercury dimes, etc.
—rolls of coins with different dates
—full-year sets (e.g., 1942 sets of dollars, halves, etc. from each mint)
—type sets (full sets of Morgan dollars, Franklin halves, etc.)
—commemorative coins (legal tender coins issued for a specific anniversary, statehood celebration, etc.)

I won't bother to give current prices here because of the rapid changes taking place in this market. But purely as an example, I bought a roll of BU Morgan silver dollars in 1976 for $120. Today they are selling for $900!

You can buy rare coins from your local coin dealer, but you'll want to compare prices and quality. I think it's probably best to deal with a large reliable firm. Prices for the same graded coin can differ substantially among dealers. The following firms specialize in rare coins:

> Numisco, Inc.
> 175 West Jackson Blvd.
> Chicago, IL 60604
> Toll-free 800-621-5272
> or in Ill. 312-922-3465

> Bowers & Ruddy
> 6922 Hollywood Blvd., Suite 600
> Los Angeles, CA 90028
> Toll-free 800-421-4224
> or in Calif. 213-466-4595

> Deak-Perera Co.
> Numismatic Division
> 630 Fifth Ave.
> New York, NY 10020
> Toll-free 800-223-5510
> or in NY, 212-757-0100

Overgrading and counterfeits are serious problems in the rare coin industry. The above dealers guarantee their coins for several years after you purchase them. You can also have your coins certified by the American Numismatic Association.

The safest place to store your coins is in a safe deposit box.

Postage stamps

Stamp collecting is the world's leading hobby. Rare stamps, like coins, have a ready market around the world. From an investment point of view, the price of rare stamps has skyrocketed. The Scott U. S. Stamp Index has leaped from a base of 100 in 1968 to over 1,000 today—an 18.8 percent compounded annual rate of appreciation!

Individual issues can still be purchased fairly cheaply. You may want to invest in international issues someday, but at first you should limit your purchases to U. S. stamps that have a proven track record. Avoid the purchase of low-value U. S. commemorative stamps touted by the post office—many sheets are actually worth less than face value to stamp collectors!

Again, stay with high-quality issues, and make sure your stamp collection is well preserved and insured. There are many auction houses in the stamp market, especially in New York (Harmers, Siegels, Stolows, etc.). You'll also find stamp dealers at many coin shows.

Before you invest in stamps, you must get a copy of *Stamps & Stories*, available at your local post office. It's a beautiful, full-color encyclopedia of U. S. stamps, containing the latest stamp prices. Cost is $3.50.

Diamonds and gems

Can the small investor still buy an investment-grade diamond? Not any more. Diamond prices have skyrocketed, and top-quality diamonds are selling for $5,000 to $10,000 a carat. Half-carat diamonds of lesser quality are still within the reach of the small investor—but you'll probably have to pay the retail jewel price. Moreover, the Gemological Institute of America (GIA), the top-rated diamond certifier, is reluctant to certify smaller stones.

But you can still get into the precious stones market. Colored gemstones are a rising investment field and are available at nearly every price level. Emeralds, sapphires, and rubies have all jumped in price to practically match that of diamonds. But while the semi-precious stones, such as aquamarine, amethyst, tourmaline, and garnet, have had rapid appreciation, too, they can still be purchased by the small investor. Prices begin as low as $100 a carat.

The investment market in gemstones is still very young, and

there are so many factors to consider in buying a gem that I don't recommend it until the small investor has become quite knowledgeable and is financially secure in other investment areas. Markups in gemstones are still high, and require long-term holding before profits can be achieved. For more information on gemstones, contact the following organizations (both recommended as reputable dealers by The Ruff Times):

Investment Rarities   H. Stern Jewelers, Inc.
One Appletree Square   645 Fifth Ave.
Minneapolis, MS 55420   New York, NY 10022
Toll-free 800-328-1928   Toll-free 800-221-4768
or 612- 853-0700 in Minn.   or 212-688-0300 in NY

Rare Books

Rare books can be an interesting investment, particularly if you enjoy reading. Quality of the cover and pages, scarcity, which edition, and fame of the author are all important factors in determining the market value of a rare book.

Certain books in good condition have appreciated steadily in value. Adam Smith's classic, *The Wealth of Nations* (first edition, London 1776) increased in value during the past decade alone from $1,400 to $8,000. Darwin's original *Origin of Species* climbed from $700 in 1970 to over $3,000 today. Other books by famous authors have done equally well.

Nevertheless, book-collecting has one major drawback for the novice. Generally rarity is the most important factor in determining demand, and that usually means that a $10,000 book will appreciate faster and be easier to sell than a $100 book! Unless you simply want to own a certain book, and look at the investment angle as a sidelight, you should probably avoid these lower-priced and less-demanded books.

Auction houses are still the best place to buy and sell rare books. Sotheby's, mentioned earlier, has catalogs on upcoming auctions. So does California Book Auction Galleries (358

Golden Gate Ave., San Francisco, CA 94102).

When searching for lower-priced books, be extremely careful. There's a lot of junk on the market—and not just in terms of content!

Autographs

Original manuscripts, letters, directives, and other material handwritten by famous people can be worth something if you find an interested buyer. Autographs vary greatly in price, depending on the movie star, sports hero, politician, author, or historical figure, as well as on *what* they wrote. Autographs have generally appreciated in price, like all collectibles. But watch out for fakes. The leading authority on autographs is Charles Hamilton, who owns his own auction house (Charles Hamilton Galleries, 25 E. 77th St., New York, NY 10021). He charges 25 percent commission, however. Sotheby's still charges only 10 percent to buy or sell autographs at its auctions.

Vintage wines

Unlike most inflation hedges that have had a steady upward trend, wines have gone through several boom-bust cycles over the past few decades. They are highly speculative. But wines continue to be a tempting investment, perhaps in part because of the allure surrounding the whole mystique of "good" wine. In the past few years auction prices have doubled for most vintages. If you can buy near the bottom of a downtrend, you can make a lot of money with just a small investment—as little as $100.

The chief source for buying and selling wine is Christie's in London (8 King St., London, England). The head of the wine department there will even make selections for you at no extra charge. Purchase the wine at auction through Christie's and have the auction house store the wine for you. (Don't take delivery—it requires too much trouble and red tape.) Christie's will bid on the wine for you and store it at a nominal fee of a few cents per case per week. When you decide to sell, the wine department will auction the wine for you, charging you a 10 percent commission. It's that simple! The value of the wine will be stated in British pounds, not U. S. dollars, so you will have to calculate changes in the exchange rate when figuring your profit (or loss). For details, write Christie's and ask for their wine brochure for American buyers.

Other Collectibles

There are hundreds of other collectibles available, although some, like classic antique cars, are too expensive or exotic for the beginner. Your best bet is to choose something you like for its intrinsic value, learn everything you can about it, and then purchase items that are high quality, rare, and decently priced. You should become familiar with the major auction houses, and be aware of current selling prices. Avoid large, cumbersome, or fragile items, or things of limited demand. Beware of con artists, counterfeits, and auction fever. And most of all, enjoy your investments!

CHAPTER 10

COMMODITY TRADING FOR THE SMALL SPECULATOR

"Now I've a sheep and a cow,
everybody bids me good-morrow."

Commodity futures trading—that is, speculating on the future price of basic commodities—is undoubtedly the *fastest* way for the small investor to pyramid a little cache into a large fortune. Millionaire writer Morton Shulman calls commodity trading the "last opportunity" for the young speculator who wants to make a killing in the market. When trading commodities, you typically put down only 5-10 percent "margin" money, which means you actually control 10-20 times the amount of your investment. You can control a $20,000 contract with as little as $1,000. Real estate and stock options may be the only other vehicles whereby you can control significant assets with just a little money down.

Suppose for instance that you expect the price of wheat to rise. You "buy long" 1,000 bushels of wheat for future delivery, say in December. If a thousand bushels of wheat has a current market value of $5,000, you will be required to put up only about $400 to control that thousand bushels of wheat. That's leverage! As we shall see, this can many times magnify your profit—or loss.

119

Now suppose that after you buy long, a wheat shortage appears, due to a sudden increase in demand by the Russians or a massive drought at harvest time. Wheat moves up in price from $5 to $6 a bushel. Your contract of 1,000 bushels has increased in value from $5,000 to $6,000—a gain of $1,000 or 20 percent of the total price. But since you only put down $400, your $1,000 profit translates into a yield of 250 percent!

On the other hand, suppose a bumper crop came in and the price of wheat fell to $4. If you were buying long, you would have *lost* $1,000, which would have wiped out your original investment ("margin") and cost you an additional $600 as well. You would have received a "margin call" asking you to put up more money immediately or your contract would have to have been liquidated.

Most novice investors can't handle this kind of fast trading. It's surely not for the fainthearted. The commodity futures market should not be considered by the beginner who has just a few thousand dollars to invest. Those with the speculative spirit may be lured by the promise of huge profits, but the realistic investor will carefully consider the risks too. I don't recommend the futures market until you have at least a $10,000 investment portfolio, and even then it should be treated as pure speculation.

Money you use to speculate in futures should be money you can afford to lose—and the brand-new investor can hardly afford to lose anything. Moreover, I have found that the broker's warning that you should "not speculate unless you can afford to lose everything" is easier to agree to than to experience. It's one thing to acknowledge the possibility of losing your hard-earned money sometime in the future, and quite another to be faced with heavy losses and gut-wrenching margin calls, especially after the broker usually follows up his warning with assurances of how profitable and foolproof his trading system has been in the past!

Four Steps to Low-risk Trading

Clearly, then, commodity trading is a highly lucrative but risky business. Fortunately, there are ways to reduce your risks, even though you can't eliminate them. Let me emphasize four important points.

First, look for commodities that are in a sideways pattern. This means that when you look at the commodity charts you will find some commodities that have maintained a fairly constant price for a period of time—its graph moves sideways. Place a buy order 5 or 10 percent above the current price, and wait for the price to move out of the sideways pattern. Or, if you think the price will break downward, you could place a sell order (called "selling short"). During a highly inflationary cycle, most breakouts move into higher levels, but don't be afraid to sell short occasionally if you think market conditions call for it.

The advantage of this approch is that you don't enter a commodity market until the price comes to you, so the trend has already begun before you buy. But you are close enough to the beginning of the trend to take full advantage of it. Another advantage of this method is that your money isn't tied up in commodity trading until it actually becomes profitable. Until your buy or sell order is exercised, your speculative funds can earn interest in a money market fund or other highly liquid vehicle.

Even volatile commodities like silver can enter into a sideways pattern for several years, although the sideways band can admittedly be rather wide. From 1975 until 1978, silver stayed within the $4 to $6 range. The patient speculator could have placed a buy order at around 10 percent above the plateau, or $6.50-$7.00, and then waited until silver broke out. While it may have been frustrating, the waiting period would have paid off handsomely. Once silver hit $7, it took off, and shot up to $45 in early 1980. You would have made spectacular profits.

It's hard to be patient and play this waiting game, especially when other commodities may be jumping around at a frenzied pace. Nevertheless, I strongly discourage new traders entering a market *after* it has risen steeply. This is a common but fatal mistake of inexperienced traders. The general public always seems to get in too late, and usually at the top. Or they sell at the bottom. Many traders, excited by daily news reports of higher prices, bought silver in early 1980 when it was close to $50 an ounce, only to see the price plummet to $10 in a matter of months! Don't let this happen to you.

Second, place a "stop loss" order as the price moves up. A "stop loss" order is an order to your broker to sell when the market reaches a certain price. If the price is never reached, then the order is never filled. "Trailing stops" are stop-loss orders that follow the rise (or fall, if you're selling short) of the price of the commodity. Trailing stop loss orders are essential to preserving your profits. They should be flexible enough to allow for small corrections, so you're not stopped out too early, but tight enough to get you out of the market before the bottom drops out. A good rule of thumb is to place stop loss orders at 10-15 percent below the current price. As profits become more substantial, you can afford to widen the stop loss order. If you had followed this pattern in silver, you probably would have gotten out at around $40 an ounce.

Third, pyramid conservatively. Pyramiding is a way to multiply your profits even further. As the price of a commodity moves up, you make more money, and your account will show a growing equity on paper. For example, if wheat increases in price from $5 to $6, your "paper profits" are $1,000 on a 1,000 bushel contract. You can then use that $1,000 to buy additional contracts.

There's a right way and a wrong way to pyramid. The right way is to add *fewer* contracts as the price climbs. If you start out with 3 contracts in wheat, you could conservatively add 1 or 2 contracts as the price moves up. The wrong way is to add 5 or 6 contracts—more than what you started with. Why? Because if the price suddenly reverses, you could lose all your profits quickly.

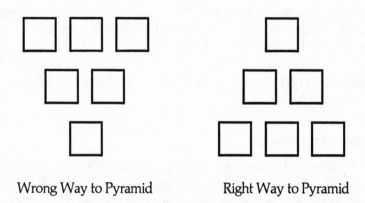

Wrong Way to Pyramid   Right Way to Pyramid

Fourth, never buy or sell a contract on a hot tip or hunch. Be rational, study your charts and the fundamental economic factors, and read the financial newspapers. Don't panic! Most importantly, be your own money manager, You don't let the grocery clerk tell you what to buy for dinner, and you shouldn't let the commodity broker tell you what to buy for investments, either. Every broker thinks he has a sure-fire way to make money in commodities. But if it doesn't work, out, *you* are the one who loses. Make your own decisions, and use your broker only for executing those decisions.

This simple approach of watching for sideways patterns and profiting from the breakouts, requires much patience. Most traders don't follow it because it means being completely out of the commodity markets from time to time. But the ones that have followed this system have profited handsomely, trading perhaps 6-7 commodities during the year, if that many.

Virtually all commodities trade in a sideways pattern at some time or another. Get some charts on commodities from your broker and take a look. It has happened to soybeans, barley, lumber, Swiss francs, sugar, copper, silver, and many others. You can be in at the beginning of next year's market phenomenon!

I don't expect you to use this approach without some additional guidance. This easy trading device has been fully developed by commodity trader Bruce Gould in his book, *My Most Successful Technique for Making Money*. You should read it carefully before trying this method. (Bruce Gould, P. O. Box 16, Seattle, WA 98111, $10).

Cost Approach

Another approach to trading commodities is the "cost method." This system is based on the theory that when the trading price of a commodity falls until it nears the price it actually costs to produce it, it won't be long before the price has to go back up. To use this method, you search for commodities that have already gone through a serious depression in prices and are close to *cost*. You buy long on contracts with the furthest delivery month available, and play a waiting game. The price is bound to rise above costs eventually, or else the producers will stop producing it.

This approach has been developed by investment advisor John Pugsley. He uses the case of copper as an example. When copper was selling for 70 cents a pound in 1978, it was close to its production cost. Within several months, the price rose and eventually reached $1.40, before dropping back again in 1980.

I personally like the Bruce Gould method best, because it allows you to earn interest on your money while you're waiting for the markets to reach your price objective. Also, if the market doesn't perform as you expect, you haven't lost anything because you haven't entered it yet. The cost approach is useful, and fairly reliable, however, and can be another source of low-risk profits.

MidAmerica Exchange: Small Speculator's Delight

The major commodity exchanges—such as the Chicago Board of Trade, the New York Mercantile Exchange, and the International Monetary Fund—allow you to trade in a variety of commodities, including agricultural commodities, metals, and financial instruments. They require fairly substantial minimum investments, which prevent most average income earners from getting into the futures market.

However, the MidAmerica Commodity Exchange in Chicago offers a unique alternative for the beginner. It provides for very small contracts in 7 commodities—cattle, hogs, soybeans, corn, oats, wheat, silver and gold. The main advantage is in MidAmerica's lower minimums. For example, while the Chicago Board of Trade has a minimum wheat contract of 5,000 bushels, MidAmerica has a 1,000-bushel contract. The initial margin requirement on CBT wheat is about $1,500, while MidAmerica's margin is only $300. The following comparison demonstrates the advantages more specifically.

Commodity	Size of Contract		Initial Margin	
	Major Exchange	MidAmerica	Major Exchange	MidAmerica
Cattle	40,000 lbs.	20,000 lbs.	$1,500	$750
Corn	5,000 bu.	1,000 bu.	$1,000	$200
Silver	5,000 oz.	1,000 oz.	$20,000	$4,000
Gold	100 oz.	33.2 oz.	$9,000	$3,000

Under these conditions, it's possible for the small trader to start speculating with $1,000. Of course, he must have additional funds to back up his margin requirements in case of a margin call. Most brokerage houses require minimum assets of several thousand dollars.

A recent study by the Commodity Futures Trading Commission showed that over 62 percent of commodity traders had less than $5,000 equity in their accounts. That would be enough for only a couple of contracts on the big boards. But, with MidAmerica, you could take several positions, make more trades, and limit your dollar commitment. Risk is a major concern in commodity trading, and mini-contracts spread that risk.

For a booklet on the MidAmerica, write:

> The MidAmerica Commodity Exchange
> 175 West Jackson Blvd.
> Chicago, IL 60604
> Telephone 312-435-0606

Once you get a better handle on commodities by trading the mini-contracts on the MidAmerica, you might try your hand at contracts on the big boards in commodities not available at the MidAmerica, such as financial instruments (Treasury bills, Ginnie Maes, etc.).

Choosing a Discount Commodity Broker

A good commodity broker, like a good stockbroker, is hard to find. You won't find many who are willing to let you trade your own way. They're after commissions, of course, and they want to demonstrate their abilities by keeping you trading one commodity after another.

Commodity brokers are paid a set commission per commodity contract, rather than a percentage of the buying or selling price. Brokers from most major firms can sometimes set their own commission rates, so see if yours is willing to negotiate.

The discounters have recently entered the commodity markets, although they are far less numerous than stock market discount houses. Here are two discount commodity brokers you may wish to check out:

> Source Commodities Corp.
> 70 Pine St.
> New York, NY 10005

Toll-free 800-221-7436
Or in New York 212-422-0598

Eastern Capital Corp.
28 State St.
Boston, MA 02109
Toll-free 800-343-7008
or in Mass. 617-227-6505

At Eastern, "round trip" commissions (flat fee charged for buying and selling a contract) are only $25, compared to $50 to $100 at most other brokerage houses.

There are risks using a discount commodity broker, however. A securities account is insured, but a commodity account is not. Recently some commodity houses have gone bankrupt, leaving many traders holding the bag. Be sure to check out the financial soundness of a discount broker before committing funds.

Managed Commodity Accounts

One other alternative for the individual speculator is to invest in a managed commodity plan. While minimum investment is $25,000 and higher for individually-managed accounts by large brokerage firms, pooled "mutual funds" in commodities typically have a $5,000 minimum. These plans offer professional management by trading experts, diversification, and spreading of risk because the money of numerous investors is pooled.

Risks are significant, nevertheless, and professional management does not guarantee profits. Many funds have performed extremely well, gaining over 100 percent a year, and then suddenly lost money. This is particularly true of computer-trading systems, which use technical data that is continually changing and thus requires frequent reevaluation. I personally prefer accounts traded on a combined technical and fundamental basis, where economic and political factors are taken into consideration.

Moreover, managed accounts are notorious for charging high management fees, commissions, and profit-sharing. So when you consider a managed account, examine the full costs of the plan—they can be substantial. In my opinion, you should be your own money manager, and trade your own account. If you say you don't have the time or the expertise, perhaps you should select another investment medium where you do have the time and knowledge for successful trading.

Most managed accounts are not available to small investors for several reasons. Minimum investment is typically $5,000, and more importantly, income and net worth minimums are required—starting at an annual income of $25,000 or a net worth of $100,000 *not* including home and automobiles!

However, I have come across an interesting managed commodity account which has a very small minimum investment and *no* income or net worth requirements. It's called SNW Commodities Ltd., which is traded out of London. Minimum investment is only $1,000, and your money is pooled with other investors for diversification of risk. SNW Commodities guarantees that you won't get a margin call, so you can't lose more than your actual investment. The commodity firm has been trading since 1974, and has had a good track record, although last year's performance was lackluster. As always, past performance is no proof of future performance.

SNW Commodities is part of the J. H. Rayner Group of Companies, which was purchased by Sunshine Mining Co., the largest silver mining operation in the United States, in 1979. The commodity firm charges an initial service fee of 5 percent, and takes 20 percent of all profits.

SNW Commodities has several advantages over U. S. markets.

In addition to the U. S. markets it also trades the London markets, which are often more liquid that the U. S. and have fewer daily limits. Trading also includes lead, tin, zinc, nickel, aluminium, rubber and wool, which are not traded in the U. S.

For a free brochure on the managed commodity program, write:

> Britannia Commodity Service Inc.
> Attn. Mr. Eric L. Clayden, President
> 8720 E. Columbus Ave.
> Scottsdale, AZ 85251
> Telephone 602-994-4414

Britiannia Commodity Service Inc. is an authorized international sales company for SNW Commodities Ltd., and is registered with the Commodity Futures Trading Commission.

A Final Word

Commodity futures trading is not for everyone, but by following the guidelines set out in this chapter you can greatly reduce the risks. Managed accounts may be a better approach for those who don't want margin calls or who don't have the time or interest to trade for themselves. Big profits are available, but it takes a strong stomach and patient fortitude to realize them!

CHAPTER 11

KEEP WHAT YOU EARN— ARE TAX SHELTERS FOR YOU?

"Beware of little expenses,
a small leak will sink a great ship."

As inflation pushes all of us into higher tax brackets, aggressive tax planning begins to play an increasing role in the financial lives of more and more Americans. Taxes are on everyone's mind today, not just on those of the rich. Despite occasional "tax cuts," the overall tax bite is growing rapidly. In 1964, for example, the average taxpayer paid 12 percent of his income for federal income taxes. Despite three tax cuts since then, today's average taxpayer pays 21 percent to the IRS. Now that inflation is skyrocketing at double digit rates, the tax burden is fast becoming unbearable. It won't be long before all Americans will be desperately searching for "loopholes" to beat the taxman.

The chart below demonstrates the increasing burden of the federal income tax structure:

Marginal Tax Rates

Taxable Income[†]	Joint Returns	Single
$0-2,100	14%	14%
$2,100-4,200	16%	18%

$4,200-8,500	18%	22%
$8,500-12,600	21%	26%
$12,600-16,800	24%	30%
$16,800-21,200	28%	34%
$21,200-31,800	37%	44%
$31,800-56,600	49%	63%
$56,600-82,200	54%	68%
$82,200-159,000	64%	70%
$159,000-212,000	70%	70%

†After all deductions and personal exemptions.

The progressive tax structure was meant to tax only the super-rich at rates of 50% or more, but as inflation pushes us into higher incomes without increasing our standard of living, it is easy to see that even the middle class will soon be paying these confiscatory rates.

To Pay Or Not to Pay?

The purpose of tax shelters is to provide a means of deferring, or postponing, your tax obligations. For example, suppose you set up an Individual Retirement Account (IRA) as a tax shelter, and deposit the maximum $1,500 allowed. The IRS allows you to subtract that $1,500 from your taxable income and you consequently pay less taxes to the government that year. How much less depends, of course, on your tax bracket. But while taxes are *deferred*, they are not eliminated. When you withdraw that money from your IRA many years later, all withdrawals will be included in your taxable income.

Most investment advisors have argued that deferring taxes is still a good idea because when you retire, your income falls and your tax bracket will be lower.

But there is another factor to consider. Inflation is getting worse and shows no signs of letting up. By the time you retire taxes will undoubtedly be higher—much higher. Therefore it could be argued that it's better to pay your taxes now and invest the remainder of your shelterable money in inflation hedges such as gold, silver, and other hard assets.

The question you must answer is this: is it worth while deferring your taxes? Or will you wind up paying more in the end?

My general rule of thumb in making this decision is this: if you're below the 50 percent tax bracket, pay the tax and invest the difference in long-term inflation hedges.

This approach has several benefits. First, you've actually minimized your taxes, by paying them now, when your tax bracket is lower.

Second, by investing in long-term inflation hedges, you earn high profits but pay no additional taxes until you actually sell the investment. More importantly, since long-term capital gains are 60 percent tax free, your tax obligation will be much lower when you do finally sell. If you're in the 50 percent tax bracket, you'll pay only 20 percent of profits in taxes. That's a very low tax rate by today's standards.

Third, you have total freedom with your after-tax money. Don't forget that tax shelters, whether they be retirement plans, annuities, or limited partnerships, restrict your ability to withdraw your money, or use it as you please. If you withdraw your tax-sheltered money early, you'll be penalized and taxed accordingly.

Since you don't reach the 40-to-50 percent tax bracket until your taxable income exceeds $30,000 a year, many readers might be able to forget about tax shelters, self-made pension plans, annuities and the like for now. Simply pay the tax and invest the difference in gold, silver, mutual funds, foreign investments, and collectibles for maximum long-term capital gains.

Still, tax rates do continue to creep up on all of us. And don't ignore your state's income taxes when figuring your overall rate—they can add plenty to your tax bill. It may not be long before your tax burden does reach the 50 percent level, if it hasn't already, and you'll want to examine some of the tax shelters mentioned below.

Individual Retirement Plans

One of the most popular tax shelters for the small investor is the individual retirement program, either Keogh for the self-employed or IRA (Individual Retirement Account) for employees who aren't covered by a pension plan.

The tax advantages of Keoghs and IRAs are these: (1) you can deduct your contributions (up to $7,500 on a Keogh, and $1,500 on an IRA) from you gross income on your tax return; (2) all dividends, interest, and capital gains are tax deferred until you withdraw your retirement funds at age 55½ or later.

But don't forget the disadvantages: (1) you can't touch the money until age 55½ without incurring heavy penalties; (2) when you finally withdraw your money, *all* profits—including long-term capital gains— are taxed at ordinary income rates! So if you invest your Keogh or IRA in gold, silver, and other inflation hedges, which would normally be 60-percent tax free, all profits will be taxed at ordinary income rates of up to 70 percent. If you take all the money out at once, you can elect a 10-year-averaging rule that might reduce your tax rates a bit, but if your profits are substantial this won't help much.

If you do open a Keogh or IRA, make sure it is a *self-directing* plan. Stay away from bank plans that restrict your funds to low-return certificates that can't keep up with inflation. Check out individual retirement plans offered by large brokerage firms, such as Merrill Lynch, Dean Witter, Bache, etc. For a small fee, they let you invest in stocks, bonds, and precious metals.

More and more banks are permitting investors to diversify their Keogh or IRA funds. It's probably best to deal with a local bank or brokerage firm, if posssible. But if not, the following financial institutions offer self-directing plans:

> Blanchard & Co.
> 8422 Oak St.
> New Orleans, LA 70118
> Toll-free 800-535-8588

Plymouth-Home National Bank
34 School St.
Brockton, MA 02403

Lincoln Trust Co.
P. O. Box 5831
Denver, CO 80217

I mention Plymouth-Home National Bank because it offers one of the lowest-cost Keogh plans in the country. While most Keogh set-ups cost at least 1% per annum in fees, Plymouth charges only 2/5th of 1% per annum (minimum $125), a substantial savings.

Because all profits from retirement accounts are taxed at ordinary income rates, I would suggest that you use them mainly for your investments that earn dividends, interest, and short-term capital gains. Don't waste your long-term gains on a Keogh or IRA. Emphasize bonds, money market funds, high-dividend-paying stocks (like South African gold shares), and no-load mutual funds for short-term trading of less than 1 year.

Incorporating

Ted Nicholas calls incorporating the "ultimate tax shelter." Federal corporate taxes are limited to a maximum of 48 percent, and are only 22 percent if corporate profits are less than $50,000. Of course, there are additional fees, higher social security taxes, and more government paperwork to consider, but most self-employed individuals can probably save taxes by incorporating.

The least expensive way to incorporate is through Ted Nicholas' organization: Enterprise Publishing Inc., Two West Eighth Street, Wilmington, DE 19801. You should also order his fine book, *How to Form Your Own Corporation for Under $50*, ($5.95 paperback). Of course, it actually costs slightly over $100 to incorporate in Delaware now, but it's still much cheaper than the

$600 to $1,000 that most attorneys will charge.

A corporate pension plan offers greater variety and many other advantages over a Keogh plan. Contributions to corporate plans are not limited to $7,500 a year as Koeghs are. You are allowed to contribute up to 25 percent of your salary to a tax-deferred pension plan, and in some cases, even more! Unlike a Keogh plan, you can be the trustee of your own pension plan, thus avoiding high administrative fees. You can also be your own custodian, so if you buy coins or other collectibles, you can store them yourself at home or in a safe deposit box. As trustee of your pension, you can invest in virtually anything—from stocks to bonds to foreign investments. Your pension plan also avoids federal estate and gift taxes.

Annuities

Today's annuities are much like tax-sheltered savings plans. They have fewer restrictions and are more liquid than ever before. Dreyfus just recently introduced one such annuity program called Rainbow, which invests your money in Dreyfus Liquid Assets, a money market fund. As an annuity, Rainbow permits you to postpone taxation on earnings from this money market fund. Dreyfus Liquid Assets is currently earning about 10½ percent per annum, and fluctuates with national interest rates. Minimum investment is only $1,500, and Dreyfus charges a 1 percent annual fee. Unlike other annuities, there is no penalty for withdrawing your money—other than the fact that accrued interest will then be taxable. You can also borrow money from a bank, using the Rainbow annuity as collateral. For a prospectus, write or call:

> The Dreyfus Rainbow
> 767 Fifth Ave.
> New York, NY 10153
> Toll-free 800-223-0982
> In New York 212-489-4900

Another annuity that offers a wider variety of investment opportunities is called Spectrum. Spectrum is administered by Massachusetts Financial Services of Boston, one of the oldest mutual fund organizations in the U. S., and is insured by Nationwide.

In addition to a money market fund, Spectrum offers you the choice of seven other mutual funds. One fund is an aggressive growth stock market fund, another is a high-grade bond fund, and so forth. When you think the stock market is ready to explode upward, you can place your funds in their equity mutual fund. If you think interest rates are going to drop suddenly, you can switch into their high-grade bond fund. And if you think the stock and bond markets are in trouble, you can switch into their money market fund for complete safety. You are your own money manager.

In addition, you can switch from one fund to another without paying any commissions, penalties or taxes! Spectrum is an excellent tool, therefore, for trading stocks, bonds, etc., without paying taxes. All taxes are postponed, except for long-term capital gains.

Spectrum is also sold by major brokerage houses, such as Merrill Lynch, Bache, Dean Witter, etc. Spectrum is a no-load variable annuity, but there is a 1.3 percent annual administrative fee. Minimum is $1,500, and you can add to it in any amount. You can use Spectrum as collateral for a loan. For further information, write:

Spectrum
Massachusetts Financial Services of Boston
200 Berkeley St.
Boston, MA 02116

Insurance companies have also developed a number of "single-premium annuities." Interest is usually figured only once every three months, and you have to begin another annuity account if you wish to add to your funds. I personally prefer Spectrum because of its flexibility. If you're interested in other plans, see my book, *New Profits From Insurance.*

Tax-Free Municipal Bond Funds

The well-to-do buy municipal bonds because they are free from federal taxes and, in most cases, from state and local taxes as well. If you're in the 50 percent tax bracket, an 8 percent return from munies translates into a 16 percent return compared to taxable investments such as corporate bonds, money market funds, and stocks. Moreover, income from municipal bonds is completely private and does not have to be reported at all on any federal tax forms. That's another reason why munies are very popular among the rich.

Municipal bonds are issued in denominations of $5,000 each, often in bearer form. Now, through the use of municipal bond funds, you can participate in lower amounts, as low as $1,000. Consider the following municipal bond funds:

Fund	Minimum	Check-writing privilege?
Lexington Tax-Free Income P. O. Box 1515 Englewood Cliffs, NJ 07632 800-526-4791 or 800-932-0838 in NJ	$1,000	Yes
Scudder Managed Municipal Bonds 175 Federal St. Boston, MA 02110 800-225-2470 or 617-482-3990 in Mass.	$1,000	No
Vanguard Municipal Bond Fund P. O. Box 1100 Valley Forge, PA 19482 800-523-7910 or 800-362-7688 in Pa.	$3,000	Yes

The Vanguard Group of municipal bond funds offers the widest variety I have found. It has 5 different municipal bond funds from which to choose: the money market portfolio (current yield, 3.2%), short-term portfolio (5.2%), intermediate-term portfolio (6.2%), long-term portfolio (7.5%), and the high-yield portfolio (7.65%). The money market portfolio has the shortest maturity and is the least risky of the funds. The higher-performing muny funds have dropped in value as interest rates moved up sharply—the shorter-maturity funds minimize that problem.

All of these funds have a check-writing privilege, a nice feature.

Tax Shelters in Limited Partnerships

Exotic tax shelters have traditionally been the exclusive domain of the rich: limited partnerships in real estate, oil and gas drilling, movies, gold mines, equipment leasing, etc.

Small residential properties, which we discussed in chapter 8, can serve as a tax shelter for the small investor. A rented house, a fourplex, or a small apartment building can shelter a great deal of income. Interest payments, fix-up costs, and depreciation can all add up to high deductions, sometimes exceeding your downpayment.

Limited partnerships in real estate involve much bigger stakes. Typically they involve million-dollar apartment complexes and require the pooling of funds from dozens of investors. To obtain the highest write-off, the promoters will often select a large residential or commercial property that is undervalued and in need of repair. This will give the limited partners fast depreciation and a heavy amount of debt from local banks. As a result, a limited partner investing $20,000 can get deductions up to $40,000—this would be considered a 2-to-1 write-off.

These kinds of real estate partnerships are only for the upper-middle class or wealthy investor who is in the 50 percent tax bracket or higher. He needs substantial write-offs, and is willing to take the risk in undervalued properties to get it. Because of the risk and high debt load, the promoters won't consider small investors. You're required to prove a net worth of several hundred thousand dollars, or a high income of $50,000 or more.

Oil and gas tax shelters might not have such stringent financial requirements, but the write-offs aren't as high either. Most oil and gas partnerships offer up to a 90 percent write-off in the first year. Minimums are sometimes as low as $5,000 per investor—so the small investor might be able to take advantage if he has the cash.

There are sizeable administrative fees. Usually the general partner takes 15 percent, and sometimes more. And remember that this kind of partnership is a long-term commitment. Most make no provisions for you to withdraw your money before the drilling is over, perhaps 10 years down the road.

Summary on Tax Shelters

Tax shelters aren't necessary for every investor. They certainly aren't for the small investor who is just starting out, or for the average wage-earner paying less than 30 percent in taxes. But as your income increases and you make money on your investments, tax shelters in pension plans, annuities, and limited partnerships begin to make sense. In every case, it's imperative that you check out the financial soundness of the shelter first, and make sure that it will make money, too, not just save you taxes.

CHAPTER 12

RISKS AND REWARDS OF LOW INTEREST LOANS

*"Buy what thou hast no need of,
and e'er long thou shalt sell thy necessaries."*

Borrowing money can be the small investor's worst enemy, or, used prudently, it can be a great benefit.

The most common financial error of millions of Americans is to get strung out on heavy consumer debt—for buying a color TV, new appliances, a new car, vacations, and other nice but unnecessary items. They buy everything they want through the cruel master of installment loans or credit cards, stretching payments so that monthly bills are minimal. With interest rates at 18 percent or higher, total payments mount up quickly, so that many people end up paying double or triple the original purchase price for these consumer items. Moreover, because credit cards and installment loans are so easy to use, most are tempted to continue buying products and services on time until they are completely snowed under. The resulting debt structure culminates in a citizenry that teeters on the brink of bankruptcy.

Consolidate Your Loans?

Consumer debt is like being in prison, and the debtor soon starts looking desperately for a way out. One common escape route is the use of consolidating loans. A finance company will agree to take all your debts for credit cards, department stores, autos, medical bills, and other payments, and lump them together into one monthly bill. By stretching the new payments out over a longer period of time, the single monthly bill is usually *lower* than the sum of all the individual monthly bills was. This lower payment schedule seems appealing, but it is also dangerously deceptive. If your repayment schedule is extended for, say 3 years, your total interest payment is then increased three times! At interest rates of 18 percent or more, this can greatly increase your total cost.

I'm not opposed to consolidating your loans *if* you use the extra money to invest in long-term inflation hedges described in this book. But if you use the consolidated loan program as a way to buy more consumer goods on credit, or even with cash, you are a financial fool, and you'll soon be in worse trouble.

If you do use a consolidating loan, try to get one from the local bank rather than from a finance company. They usually charge less interest—perhaps 12-15 percent on personal loans.

The ultimate solution is to avoid using credit to buy any consumer items. Don't buy a TV, stereo, appliance, furniture, or other household item until you've saved up enough money to buy it outright with cash. If you don't have enough, buy second-hand goods or do without. Reread the chapter on budgeting if necessary.

Borrowed money should be used very judiciously, and seldom on consumer products. A car and a home are probably the only exceptions. There may be some unusual low-risk investment situations, however, where borrowing money may be advantageous. For example, several years ago when gold was selling for $220 an ounce, market conditions indicated that gold was going to move up sharply. At the time, I didn't have the ready cash to invest heavily, and I didn't want to liquidate other investments I held at that time. I was expecting to receive several thousand dollars in income within a few months. So I took out a personal loan, paying 12 percent annual interest, and invested it in gold. Within 2 months, gold had jumped to $300 an ounce, and was headed higher. When the expected income arrived I paid off the loan. This is what I mean by judicious use of borrowed money: loans should be *short-term*, for a low-risk *investment*, with a specific source for *repayment*.

Poor Man's Guide to Easy Loans

The wealthy investor has always had it easy when it comes to getting a loan. Knowing the bank manager personally, the wealthy investor can draw upon large lines of credit at a moment's notice to invest in anything he wants without having to convince a loan officer of the soundness of the venture and often at much more favorable terms than the small investor. As one of the bank's best corporate customers, he is charged the "prime rate," a special low-interest rate, available only to top businesses and investors. Often the rich investor is able to borrow money without putting up any collateral, and can overdraw his checking account without penalty and without paying any interest.

Meanwhile, the small struggling entrepreneur might have great difficulties in getting a loan, even with collateral. His financial condition will be checked closely, and his reason for wanting the loan must be justified. He might be turned down for the smallest of reasons. If he does get the loan, he might be charged "prime rate" plus two points, and be required to pay the loan back within a short period of time.

Fortunately, things have changed radically in the past decade. Loose banking practices have now reached the poor man's door! Recently commercial banks have begun offering overdraft checking accounts and executive lines of credit to average customers at low interest rates. Obtaining an overdraft checking account has become as easy as getting a credit card. A revolution has struck the banking community, and it is spreading like wildfire.

Overdraft checking is simple. Once you are approved you receive a checkbook from the bank, and you write yourself a loan, up to your credit limit, whenever the need arises. When the check clears, the bank pays the check, and starts charging you interest (anywhere from 12 to 18 percent depending on the bank). The bank sends you a monthly statement, declaring how much you borrowed, and how much you owe the bank on a monthly basis.

Overdraft checking has these advantages:

(1) You can use the money for any purpose. You can buy gold, or buy a used car—it's completely up to you. Talk about loose banking!

(2) Repayment schedules are very flexible, as with credit cards. I would recommend that you borrow only short term, however, and pay off loans as quickly as possible.

(3) Applying is simple. You don't even have to go into the bank! You can get an application by mail. Credit is at your fingertips when you want it. You don't have to reveal to the bank what you plan to use the money for.

(4) These are personal loans. You're not required to have co-signers or collateral to back up the loan.

(5) Insurance against bad times. The worst time to go to the bank for a loan is when you really need it! The overdraft account won't cost you anything until you actually use it.

Overdraft checking has one serious disadvantage. It may be too much of a temptation for those who can't handle credit and get easily overextended. If you are a debtaholic, stay on the wagon and avoid even investment debt. But overdraft checking is a great thing to have for those who can let it stand idle until the proper need comes along. Maintain the account only for emergencies.

I've written extensively on the many uses of overdraft checking in my book, *The Insider's Banking & Credit Almanac.* (Alexandria

House Books, 901 N. Washington St., Suite 605, Alexandria, VA 22314, $14.95).

You should check in your local area first for banks that offer overdraft accounts, either through checking accounts or your credit card. American Express offers "executive credit" loans of up to $5,000 through participating banks. Diner's Club offers "Cash Advantage" overdraft accounts to its customers nation-wide through Chase Manhattan Bank (up to $15,000 at 12 percent interest). You probably need a salary of at least $20,000 to be accepted, however. Check local telephone numbers for Diner's Club or American Express for further details.

Overdraft checking is also available nationwide through a Visa card, distributed by National Bank of North America. They offer cash advance checks at a low 12 percent interest rate. Write National Bank of North America Visa Card, P. O. Box 469, Huntington Station, NY 11746.

Citibank's nationwide Visa also offers cash advances, but they do not have the check-writing feature. You must go to a participating bank personally in order to obtain the cash advance. Interest rates are low (12 percent or less). Write Citibank Visa, P. O. Box 900, Huntington Station, NY 11746.

CHAPTER 13

INVEST IN YOURSELF— THE REWARDS OF A SMALL BUSINESS

"Keep thy shop, & thy shop will keep thee."

The final area of investment that I will cover in this book is one that can be highly speculative—or extremely conservative. It can double your money overnight, or take years before it begins to pay off. It can require hours of work each day, or just a little thought and delegation of authority.

The advantages are many. Through careful planning, you can defer taxes on all your earnings—almost indefinitely. When you do finally pay taxes, it's at low, favorable rates. There are no minimums, maximums, or margin calls. You can pyramid your profits with very little risk. And you can earn money doing something you really enjoy.

Investing in yourself can be a source of great personal satisfaction as well as a source of profits. Money is a great reward for having chosen wise investments, but it can't match the joy that comes from knowing you are a personal success in your own business.

Many people may well find that investing in themselves is more profitable and more fulfilling than investing in gold, silver, mutual funds, or foreign currencies. Many small investors are taking their hard-earned savings and investing in education, to secure a promotion, to learn a technical skill, to purchase a franchise, or to start a new business—all in an effort to be better off both financially and emotionally.

In today's uncertain world, it pays to learn a second trade or job skill. The economy is on a boom-bust roller coaster ride, and no one's job is absolutely secure. Consequently, it's extremely important that you establish a savings program, build up your food supply, and seek out new business opportunities from time to time.

Outlook for Small Business

There are numerous business opportunities that don't require a lot of money up front. Since this is something that will involve a lot more of your time than will most investments, make sure you choose something you like, and not just something with the highest profit motive.

Consider the following opportunities today:

Learn a new skill. There will always be a heavy demand for competent artisans and repairmen in almost every field. Learning to build cabinets, repair plumbing, upholster furniture, fix cars, photograph children, or type legal drafts can provide a sizeable second income, reduce your own repair bills, and give you a tangible insurance policy against bad times.

Sell unique information. The business of selling information and ideas is booming. Everyone has specialized knowledge of some sort, whether it's a unique recipe, a new way to make money, a way to improve office efficiency, or a better way to raise children. Packaging this information can take many forms—cassette tapes, books, newsletters, seminars, and television programing are just a few. The mail order business, in particular, can provide an easy way to get started fast and with little capital investment. Many shrewd entreprenuers with a marketable idea have started with just a $10 ad in the classified section of a newspaper or magazine, and turned it into thousands of dollars in surprisingly short time.

Become a salesman. Selling cosmetics, encyclopedias, cleaning products, or vitamins to your friends and neighbors may seem pedestrian to some, but it may be right for you. It is highly competitive, and high volume is essential to success. Some people are born salesmen, and could sell a glass of ice water to an Eskimo. Others would have difficulty selling water to a man who has been lost in the desert for three days. If you have an easy way of talking with people, a creative flair for advertising, a way of judging other people's needs, and have a product you honestly believe in, you may be able to join the hundreds of men and women who have become millionaires through direct sales.

Buy a franchise. Franchises are springing up all over the country, in everything from fast food to ladies' underwear. As a franchise owner you receive the benefits of national advertising, a ready market, and sometimes instant recognition. But stick with the proven performers when selecting a specific franchise. And beware of promoters promising quick profits. Too often the profits are all made by the franchise sellers, not the franchise owners.

Become a broker. As more people enter the market for the first time, business is booming in the major brokerage houses, where stocks, coins, collectibles, and other investments are bought and sold. Most brokerage firms offer their own educational facilities for beginning employees, or for those who want to work part-time.

Become a consultant. This is another fast-growing area that deserves looking into, particularly for those who have chosen early "retirement." If you've led a distinguished career in government service, or achieved success in a large corporation, you may have special inside knowledge that other companies desperately need and are willing to pay big money for. Several courses are advertised in the *Wall Street Journal* telling you how to become a profitable consultant.

For More Information

Many books and articles have been written on the subject of small business. One of the largest organizations that offers detailed information on various self-employment opportunities is the American Entrepreneurs Association (2311 Pontius Ave., Los Angeles, CA 90064), headed by self-made millionaire Chase Revel. His organization puts out hundreds of special reports on individual entrepreneur-oriented businesses, such as mail order, consulting, car washes, tax preparation, etc. Most of the time, I think the reports are shallow and not worth the money, but some reports might give you some ideas.

AEA has a better service in their monthly magazine, *Entrepreneur* (same address, $72 a year), which updates you on new business opportunities.

Al Lowry's new book, *How You Can Become Financially Successful By Owning Your Own Business* (Simon & Schuster, 1981), is very helpful in setting up a new business, or for those who already own a business. His book should be available in the major bookstores.

One Final Warning

Make sure you test the market, if possible, before spending a lot of money in your part-time business. I've known of too many cases where people lost everything they had in a no-win venture because they risked too much money on an unproven project. You can lose big money speculating in the investment field, but you can lose it just as fast in franchises, new ventures, and bad loans. Remember that there can be *two* reasons why no one else is selling your idea or product yet: either they haven't thought of it, or they realized that there is little demand for it.

Choose a business that doesn't require a great deal of capital investment at first. Then, once you've tested the waters and your business is established, you can expand and invest more.

CHAPTER 14

YOUR INVESTMENT PORTFOLIO— FROM $100 TO $1,000

*"Great estates may venture more;
little boats must keep near shore."*

Now we come to the most important chapter. What kind of investments are suitable at different levels of income and net worth?

I created the $100 investment portfolio to prove a point. Today the world of high finance is available to *all* investors, not just the rich. Even a student living on a very low budget can take advantage of precious metals, the stock market, and money market funds! While the $100 investment portfolio is suitable for all investors, at any level of income, it is fairly conservative, emphasizing steady, long-term gains.

Many investors, of course, want more out of their investment program, so I've also developed alternatives for the $500 portfolio, as well as the $1,000, $2,500, $5,000, and $10,000 levels. These are, of course, merely guidelines for diversification; your personal portfolio may vary according to your desires.

At larger portfolio levels, the choice of investments is rather numerous. It won't be possible to invest in all the alternatives available. Therefore, I've listed in italics those investments that I would consider "optional."

153

The $100 Investment Portfolio

For the rock-bottom beginning investor, I would recommend the following no-minimum investments:

> Individual silver dimes or quarters (pre-1965)
> Money market funds (Alliance Capital Reserves or American Liquid Trust)
> Equity mutual fund (Twentieth Century Select Investors)
> *Swiss franc savings account (Migros Bank or Cantonal Bank in Zurich)*

You could divide the portfolio equally for maximum diversification, but you may want to make adjustments, to take advantage of a rising stock market or falling interest rates, for example. I have purposely avoided assigning specific percentages to individual portfolios because investors have different goals and attitudes. One investor may feel uncomfortable investing in stocks or gold, and may wish to keep all of his funds in a money market fund. Others may wish to speculate entirely in fast-moving markets.

Note that the Swiss franc savings program is in italics, meaning that it is optional. At this low savings level, it probably pays to wait before sending money overseas.

This $100 investment portfolio has had a remarkable performance record over the past decade, yielding over 15 percent a year.

The $500 Investment Portfolio

The $500 portfolio permits a little more variety in your investments. Consider:

> A small gold coin, or gold bullion (Merrill Lynch Gold Sharebuilders fund)
> Silver dollars, halves, quarters or dimes

Money market funds
Equity mutual funds (Energy Fund, Guardian Mutual Fund, Twentieth Century Funds)
Swiss franc savings account

If you're going to buy gold at this level, I recommend Merrill Lynch's gold bullion fund rather than buying a coin because of the high premium charged for small coins. Merrill Lynch, on the other hand, charges a low 5½ percent commission. Also, avoid numismatic coins at this point because of high cost.

The $1,000 Investment Portfolio

The $1,000 portfolio allows you to branch out a bit further.

Gold coins, or gold bullion (Merrill Lynch)
"Junk" silver coins
Money Market funds
Equity mutual funds
Swiss franc savings accounts
Numismatic silver coins
Gold shares mutual funds (United Services Fund or Golconda)

At this stage you could also start a coin-of-the-month purchase plan. Note that I've italicized two investments as optional at this level—numismatic silver coins and gold mutual funds.

The $2,500 Investment Portfolio

At the $2,500 level, you should put at least half your money into what I consider the "basics," listed in the $100 portfolio, and choose one or two of the higher-yielding but somewhat more risky areas for the rest.

Gold bullion coins and "junk" silver coins
Money market funds
Equity mutual funds

Swiss franc savings accounts
Numismatic coins
Family of mutual funds (Dreyfus, Scudder, Rowe-Price, etc.)
Gold shares mutual funds
A few collectibles (stamps, art, rare books, etc.)

Once you've invested in a family of mutual funds, you should take advantage of the telephone-switch service to maximize profits.

The $5,000 Investment Portfolio

At the $5,000 stage, you are ready to expand further into the non-traditional markets, such as collectibles and foreign stock markets. However, I still list both of these areas as optional. Maintain your foundation in the basics, both for security and liquidity.

Bullion coins, rare coins, gold bullion
Money market funds
Equity mutual funds (gold, family of funds, etc.)
Swiss franc savings account
Collectibles
Foreign stock mutual funds (Templeton, Scudder's International Fund, etc.)

The $10,000 (or more) Investment Portfolio

Only at the $10,000 level should you begin to speculate in commodity futures, the Eurocurrency markets, real estate, gemstones and tax shelters. All of these are listed as optional, however. You should also consider overdraft checking accounts for back-up emergencies, or for short-term investing needs. Again, I would recommend placing half the money in bullion coins, money market funds, equity mutual funds, and Swiss francs for long-term appreciation, and the remainder in other speculative ventures.

Bullion coins, rare coins, gold bullion
Money market funds
Mutual funds (gold, equities, foreign markets, families of funds)
Eurocurrency accounts (Swiss francs, German marks, British pounds, U. S. dollars, etc.)
Collectibles
Gemstones (colored stones, small diamonds, etc.)
Real estate investments
Commodity trading (beginning with MidAmerica Exchange)
Managed commodity accounts
Tax shelters (annuities, municipal bond funds, limited partnerships)

It's unlikely that you'll be able to fit all of the above investment vehicles into a $10,000 investment portfolio—you'll have to select several alternatives that suit your tastes. Spread your risks by not investing more than 25 percent in any one category. As long as inflation and economic crises continue, gold and silver should remain a part of your investment portfolio—25 percent is not too much. Among all the investments mentioned above, the precious metals have proven to be extremely profitable and the best performers during an inflationary climate.

CHAPTER 15

HOW TO KEEP
UP TO DATE

"The used key is always bright."

The world of high finance is a world of rapid change. All the investments that I've mentioned or recommended in this book go through cycles, moving up and down with such changes in the economic climate as the rate of inflation, interest rates, etc. I've emphasized liquidity in your investments so that you can switch easily from one investment to another (or, for safety, into a money market fund), by telephone, writing a check, or mailing a letter.

There are many books, magazines, and newsletters that will keep you abreast of current trends or new approaches to the investment world. In this chapter, I've tried to mention as many *inexpensive* sources of information as possible.

Newsletters and Magazines

Mark Skousen's Forecasts & Strategies is my own monthly financial letter (Phillips Publishing, Inc., 7315 Wisconsin Ave., NW, Suite 1200N, Washington, D. C. 20014, $95 a year). My letter covers the economy, world events, and how taxes and inflation affect your investments. It's a "how to" letter with lots of specifics. Naturally, I consider it to be the best letter on the market today.

The Ruff Times (Target Publishers, P. O. Box 2000, San Ramon, CA 94583, $125 a year) offers excellent services for the small investor. The subscription price includes: 12 months of the *Ruff Times*, Howard Ruff's entertaining and useful newsletter (published every two weeks); a copy of Howard's encyclopedic *Howard Ruff From A to Z*; and most importantly, a toll-free number for personal investment counseling with financial experts. I serve as a special consultant to the *Ruff Times* member services. You can charge your subscription to your credit card (but reread the chapter on debt first!) by calling toll-free 800-227-0703, or in California 800-642-0204. Ruff Times also puts on the least expensive investment seminars—only $95 for three days of expert advice.

Personal Finance (Kephart Communications, Inc., 901 N. Washington St., Suite 605, Alexandria, VA 22314, $65 for 24 issues a year) is the best newsletter for all around coverage in the field of investments and taxes. Articles are written by many top experts, not just by one writer. I write a regular column for *PF* and serve as a consulting editor. For the price, this is the best newsletter offering specific recommendations (it's registered as an investment advisor with the Securities & Exchange Commission). *PF*'s sister publication, *Tax Angles*, is also highly recommended for those of you facing a growing tax burden.

Gold Newsletter (National Committee For Monetary Reform, 8422 Oak St., New Orleans, LA 70118, $39 a year) offers interesting articles related to gold as an inflation hedge.

Changing Times (Editors Park, MD 20782, $12 a year) is the bargain magazine anywhere—at $1 a copy, it can't be beat. It contains a lot of practical financial information—highly recommended!

Most of the above recommended newsletters and magazines aren't available on the newstands. Financial publications such as

Money magazine, *Barrons, Forbes,* and the *Wall Street Journal* can be read at your local library.

Books

I would recommend the following books for additional investment advice:

The Alpha Strategy, by John A. Pugsley (Common Sense Press, 711 West 17th St., Costa Mesa, CA 92627, $10) is an excellent way to beat inflation, taxes and shortages—especially for the small investor. The approach is simple—stockpile basic consumer goods before you need them! In his book Pugsley lists items you need to store.

How to Prosper During the Coming Bad Years, by Howard J. Ruff (Times Books, Three Park Ave., New York, NY 10016, $8.95). This bestseller is full of helpful advice for those who are just starting out financially. It is an unorthodox approach that will get you through the eighties in prosperity.

What Has Government Done to Our Money?, by Murray Rothbard (LF Books, 206a Mercer St., New York, NY 10012, $3) is a primer that will tell you more about the cause of our economic problems than any other book today—in only 62 pages! Highly recommended!

INDEX

OTHER BOOKS BY MARK SKOUSEN

Playing the Price Controls Game. This book deals with the number one problem facing our country today: government control over prices, wages, rents, and our financial lives. This book, already in its fourth printing and selected as the book of the month by the Conservative Book Club, offers practical advice on how to prepare for and even profit from coming wage and price controls. This book is available for $10.95 from:

> Arlington House
> 333 Post Road West
> Westport, CT 06880

The 100 Percent Gold Standard. This book is the only volume on the market today which describes in detail the history of the hard-money school, those economic thinkers and political leaders who supported a pure gold standard of money. They included such people as Thomas Jefferson, John Adams, F. A. Hayek, and Murray N. Rothbard. This book also covers the economic and political arguments in favor of and against the gold standard. It is available for $10 from:

> University Press of America
> 4720 Baston Way
> Lanham, MD 20801

Mark Skousen's Complete Guide to Financial Privacy. Your financial affairs are open to the increasing threat of lawsuits, government snooping, and robbery. Learn how to protect what you've earned! Available for $14.95 postpaid from:

> Alexandria House Books
> 901 N. Washington, St., Suite 605
> Alexandria, VA 22314

The Insider's Banking and Credit Almanac. This is a consumer's guide to the "unseen revolution" in banking and credit. *The Almanac* reveals the inside secrets of personal finance—"The Perfect Loan" (how to borrow $25,000 overnight), high earnings on your checking account and savings accounts, foreign bank accounts, smart ways to take advantage of credit cards, how to start your own bank, and how to determine the safety of your bank. Available for $14.95 from:

> Alexandria House Books
> 901 N. Washington St., Suite 605
> Alexandria, VA 22314

New Profits From Insurance. This book reveals the revolution taking place in the field of annuities ("how to invest in stocks, bonds, and money market funds tax-free"), low-cost term insurance, foreign insurance plans, etc. Names and addresses of top insurance companies included. Available for $10 from:

> Mark Skousen
> P. O. Box 611
> Merrifield, VA 22116